## PREVIOUS BOOKS BY GARY PLAYER

*GARY PLAYER'S GOLF CLINIC*
*GARY PLAYER ON FITNESS & SUCCESS*

# GOLF

## PLAYING THE LIFETIME GAME

To Hector

Not only an appropriate title
but you will find that the author,
never short of an opinion, has many
sound suggestions.

From now the word 'cant' is
expunged from your life.

Enjoy and remember, the more you
practice the luckier you get. (ibid)

Happy birthday

Anne & Charles P

# GOLF BEGINS AT 50

# BEGINS AT 50

## BETTER THAN EVER

BY **GARY PLAYER**

WITH *DESMOND TOLHURST*

*STANLEY PAUL*

LONDON   SYDNEY   AUCKLAND   JOHANNESBURG

*Stanley Paul & Co. Ltd.*

*An imprint of Century Hutchinson Ltd*

*62–65 Chandos Place, London WC2N 4NW*

*Century Hutchinson Australia (Pty) Ltd*
*89–91 Albion Street*
*Surry Hills, NSW 2010*

*Century Hutchinson New Zealand Limited*
*PO Box 40–086, Glenfield, Auckland  10*

*Century Hutchinson South Africa (Pty) Ltd*
*PO Box 337, Bergvlei 2012, South Africa*

*First published in USA by Simon & Schuster Inc 1988*
*First published in Great Britain 1988*

*Printed and bound in Great Britain by*
*Butler & Tanner Ltd, Frome and London*

*ISBN 0 09 172647 6*

*Dedicated*
*to my wife, Vivienne,*
*and my six children*
*for all the love they have given me*

Vivienne and Gary Player.

# ACKNOWLEDGMENTS

"THE HARDER I PRACTICE THE LUCKIER I GET."

I've said that so often that that saying has been attributed to me. I believe it accurately reflects a cornerstone of my philosophy of life — hard work, determination, and a striving for excellence in all the things I do. Having said that, however, I must admit that luck does sometimes play a major part in success, and I've been very fortunate in that God has blessed me with such wonderful people in my life.

My wife, Vivienne, has made tremendous sacrifices throughout my professional career, which has taken me all over the globe. The wives of American tour professionals probably think that their men travel extensively. However, it was recently calculated that since 1955, when I first left my native South Africa to seek my fortune as an international professional golfer, I've traveled round the world fifty-four times, some 6.5 million miles in all, and have, effectively, sat in an airplane seat for 2.7 years of my life. I've also hit some 6.7 million golf balls!

Much of the time that I've been doing this, Vivienne has had to carry on alone, running our home and caring for our children, while I've been as much as 10,000 miles away. At other times, she's had to organize the traveling we've done together, which in earlier days included the children, a nurse and thirty-three pieces of baggage!

She's never complained. On occasions she's even claimed to have enjoyed all of this. What a wife! What a mother! If it's true that a man's success depends on having a sound and stable marriage, then we are the living proof of that. My success is our success.

I've been blessed with the support of my wonderful sister, Wilma, who has helped me for all these years.

I've also been blessed in my business associates, particularly in my close relationship with Mark McCormack. It all began with a handshake in May, 1960, and since then Mark has been in my corner both in business and also as a personal friend.

In regards to the preparation of this book, I'd especially like to thank Shaun Rowe for his fine action photographs; Dom Lupo, whose masterly illustrations of my thoughts on the game are such a great asset; and Alastair Johnston, whose enthusiasm generated the seeds of this book and without whom it would probably never have been written.

Finally, I want to thank Desmond Tolhurst, who has done such an excellent job of putting these thoughts on paper.

*GARY PLAYER*

# CONTENTS

*INTRODUCTION:*

# YES, YOU CAN

To HEAR MOST SENIOR GOLFERS TALK, you'd think it inevitable that, as you get older, your game must deteriorate. I play with a lot of middle-aged golfers in pro-ams. This is what I hear:

"I can't hit my woods (or irons) as I used to";

"When I was a kid, I'd have got it up and down. I can't do that now";

"I can't hit the ball hard any more. It hurts my back";

"I can't putt worth a lick";

"I just can't concentrate any more."

You'll note that all these statements include the word "can't." That word is no longer in my vocabulary, and it shouldn't be in yours, either. Here's why.

When I was growing up, my elder brother Ian was a tremendous influence in my life. To keep fit, he was very keen on running, and had a regular course he'd run from our home. He kept at it even though his right knee had been badly smashed up in a climbing accident when he was twelve.

One day when I was about ten, he took me on a mile run. He kept pushing me on and made no allowance for my young age or lack of size. About half a mile into the run, I gave up, saying, "I can't go any farther."

Ian got very angry at this, and told me, "Never let me hear you say, 'can't' again." He punctuated this admonition with a tremendous boot to my rear end.

Naturally, I wasn't too pleased, but I did complete that mile.

Ever since, if I've ever been tempted to say, "I can't," I feel that kick again! I then mentally draw a firm line through the "'t," and that leaves "I can."

Now let's apply this philosophy to the golf game of the typical fifty-year old—or older—who "can't" play as he or she used to. Let's strike out those "'t"'s and see what should be done.

The solutions are really very simple. First, you must ensure that your golf game is sound. Second, take steps to remain fit and strong, both mentally as well as physically.

The foundation of a sound game is a good address position. Yet, it never ceases to amaze me how many seniors have apparently never bothered to acquire a good grip, body alignment, or a proper setup to the ball. Still less do they think of checking all those aspects of their address if their games go sour. In fact, that's the first place they should look.

When golfers ask me, "What's wrong with my swing, Gary?" nine times out of ten the main flaw can be found in their grip, stance, ball position or posture. That's how important the static fundamentals are.

I don't mean to imply by this that swing fundamentals are not important. Far from it. In fact, the changes I've made during the last few years in my own swing are just what I needed and just what most seniors probably should adopt.

Many older golfers are plagued with lower back pain. Often, this is attributed to aging. However, when I got back pain myself in 1970, I knew I was pretty fit, and this put me onto one of the key causes of the problem—the type of swing I had been using.

Like most golfers, I had adopted the modern "Square-to-Square" type of swing. After much experimentation and research, I realized that this swing was a "young man's" method and was putting too much strain on my back. Yet, because the swing had received so much publicity, golfers had come to believe that it was the very best swing. However, in my opinion, playing "Square-to-Square" is absolutely the worst thing any golfer can do.

Around that time, I played some exhibitions with Billy Casper and I saw how his right foot dragged through the shot after impact. I found that this action eased the strain on my back, and from there it was a natural progression to what everybody now calls my "Walk-Through" swing. It was at this point that I met a young English professional called Peter Beames, who hounded me constantly about golf technique. He had spotted my "Walk-Through" action, and we had long discussions about it. Peter in fact wrote a book about my new swing, which he called *Walk Thru to Par*. Today, he is the only teaching professional I know of who teaches this type of swing.

I'll go into swing fundamentals in more detail in the next few chapters, but for now let me say that the swing I developed—the open to shut "Walk-Through" swing—gives me, if anything, just as much power and accuracy as before, with no strain on the back. It will, I'm sure, do the same for you.

Then there's technique in various situations: I see so many seniors who seem to have little idea of how they should adapt their swings to the differing sorts of lies they encounter on the course.

A very good example of this is sand play. Unless the player is a low handicapper, the attempts the average senior makes at recovering from sand can most charitably be described as pathetic. Yet, as I'll show you later, getting the ball out of a trap is easy once you know, and apply, the correct techniques.

I think the reason why so many seniors are at sea on such specialty shots is because it seldom occurs to them to have a lesson of that sort from their professional. If they do take a lesson, it's only to get a quick "fix" for a problem with their swing. I do remember this: When I was a young professional, I gave thousands of lessons. Even in those days, I was reckoned an excellent sand player. Yet I never once was asked to give a sand lesson!

At any rate, later in this book I'll cover thoroughly all the techniques you'll need, not only for sand but such points as maneuvering the ball, trouble shots, and so on. I also have some ideas on simplifying the short game that I think you'll find helpful.

The second part to the solution is what the Romans called *mens sana in corpore sano*—a healthy mind in a healthy body. I've been a firm believer in this from my earliest days.

In one way, my small stature has helped me here. It has always spurred me to work harder than others at developing strength and flexibility so that I could compete successfully. With my schedule, this has not been easy to do.

I remember the first time I came to America to play in the Masters, in 1957. I found that, despite all the bodybuilding I had done, I still couldn't reach the par 5s at Augusta with my second shots. In contrast, the top American pros had no difficulty getting home in two. I realized that I would never win the tournament unless I could improve the length of my wood shots.

I was very tempted to say to myself, "Well, you just can't win here." Then, that boot in the pants long ago came to my aid again and I took the necessary steps to gain distance, using more weight lifting and stretching the length of the swing.

Since then, I've won the Masters three times. My latest win came in 1978, when I was forty-two years old. This made me the oldest winner at that time.

As I've gotten older, I've realized the importance of hanging on to the strength that I've developed.

I've thought about those champions who neglected to keep themselves fit, and how they always paid the price in the end. I've also reflected on those champions who have won when most people would have thought them well over the hill.

Consider the oldest champions in golf's major championships. The list is quite instructive. Old Tom Morris last won the British Open in 1867, when he was forty-six. Julius Boros won the PGA Championship in 1968, when he was forty-eight. In 1986 two new records were set: Jack Nicklaus won the Masters at age forty-six, and Ray Floyd the U.S. Open, at forty-three. If gerontologists are correct in their assessment of the aging process, some day a man of sixty will win a major championship.

Then there's Sam Snead. Sam has had an incredible career, including a record eighty-four PGA Tour victories. However, I would imagine that the two achievements that make him proudest are those that demonstrate his longevity as a first-class golfer. He became the oldest winner on the PGA Tour when, at age fifty-two years and ten months, he won the 1965 Greater Greensboro for the eighth time (another record). He also holds the record as the youngest professional to shoot his age. He achieved this feat when, at age sixty-seven, he scored a 67 in the second round and a 66 in the last round of the 1979 Quad Cities Open.

The ladies have also set some wonderful records. For example, JoAnne Carner became the oldest winner on the LPGA Tour when she won the 1985 Safeco Classic at forty-six years of age. Also, in 1985, Kathy Whitworth at age forty-five recorded her eighty-eighth win at the United Virginia Bank Classic in a still-continuing career that started in 1958.

These great champions prove that working at your fitness pays off. They also demonstrate that there's a balance between youth and age. The young player has strength and energy, but envies the experience of the older player. The typical fifty-year-old envies the young man's fitness.

However, I've come to the conclusion that the advantage is with the older player if he or she will but realize it. Youth can't buy age's experience, but older players can retain their strength if they're prepared to work, say fifteen minutes to half an hour a day several times a week.

The yoga masters believe that chronological age means nothing as long as you retain the characteristics of youth—strength and flexibility. I agree.

I've deliberately given quite a variety of exercises in this book. What suits one person may not suit another. However, what I've given will enable any person to build up a personal program that will maintain the body in excellent condition.

I also believe that the methods you use to keep fit should be simple and not require equipment that you can't readily buy or improvise at home. The easier it is for you to get started and see results, the more likely you are to continue.

Crossing out the " 't" in "can't" is equally important on the mental side. To a large extent you are what you imagine yourself to be. The mind is an extremely powerful tool for success, but like any other tool, it has to be used. Einstein said we only use ten percent of our own brain. So there's great room for improvement. The mind must be exercised, also, and in a variety of ways.

One of the ways in which you can fulfill your goals as a golfer is by using what psychologists call "self-talk," that is, what we say to ourselves. I shall have more to say on this later, but for now let me tell you that, as a young man, I stood in front of a mirror and said to myself, "You're the greatest golfer in the world" hundreds of times. I wasn't the greatest golfer in the world at that time. Indeed, although I've had a gratifying career to date, some would say I'm still not the greatest golfer in the world.

Of one thing I'm sure. I would never have achieved a fraction of what I have done if I hadn't talked to myself in this way.

If there had been a "can't" in there, you might never have heard of me!

That is why a few years ago I was most interested in the work of a group of American psychologists who believe in the power of implanting positive suggestions in the subconscious. In fact, they are helping golfers to do what I have been doing all my life.

It's worth pointing out that the mental techniques I'll describe later will undoubtedly help your golf if you practice them. However, you also can use them in other sports or even in your business. They're universal techniques, not merely golf techniques.

I've also included some thoughts on yoga. For those of you unfamiliar with yoga, let me say it is a complete system, designed to give you the ultimate in mental and physical fitness. I studied it as a young man, and still include yoga exercises in my own regimen. I have learned much from it.

It's worth pointing out that yoga is thousands of years old. The first writings on the subject, by Patanjali, date from about 200 B.C. However, according to the German professor Max Mueller, yoga is about 6,000 years old. Nothing that didn't work could have lasted that long! That's what I told myself when I began my study of yoga, although at the time it was still much mistrusted in the West as an occult Eastern practice unsuited for Occidentals; so much so that one exercise book published a few years ago used yoga exercises from beginning to end without once acknowledging the source!

Today, happily, there are many good Western teachers of yoga. They make it easy to understand so that it is readily available to all.

One thing I'll promise you: If you do what I suggest in this book, you'll hit the ball farther, enjoy better technique, and probably feel fitter than you've felt since you were a youngster. Life, as well as golf, will be far more fun.

# CHECK YOUR GAME

CHAPTER ONE

# *THE TWO AGES*
# *OF THE SWING*

GOLF IS THE ONLY GAME I know of where, as you get to senior status, you can make adjustments that enable you to keep up with the youngsters. In tennis, a youngster no better than you were at his age would blow you away. In running, there's no such thing as a handicap in the hundred-yard dash, but that's what would be necessary to make things at all close. In golf, however, you can—and should—make some adjustments in the swing that served you as a younger player, and they will keep you in the ball game.

These changes basically fall into two categories. First, you must learn to draw the ball. Second, you must change to a swing that not only gives you power and accuracy, but also won't hurt your back, the Achilles' heel of most seniors.

## DRAW THE BALL

THERE'S no doubt in my mind that the shot with a hook/draw shape, one that moves the ball from right to left, is much stronger than the fade/slice shape that moves from left to right. Off the tee, the draw will go some 15–20 yards farther than a fade, and it's roughly one club stronger with an iron.

It's quite easy to see why this is so. If you fade/slice, the clubface is open at impact. The ball slides across the clubface, and you never compress it fully. In contrast, when you hook, the clubface is closed. You trap the ball, and compress it even more strongly than on a straight shot.

As a senior, you can't afford needlessly to give away distance. That's why you'll often hear me say, "Hook and you'll hang in there. Fade and you'll fade away." Every successful senior golfer I've met obeys this dictum.

Of the modern greats, only Lee Trevino ever faded the ball. Today, he aims less to the left, uses a metal wood, and hits the ball virtually straight with only a very slight fade. All the rest, including Sam Snead, Bobby Locke, Jack Nicklaus, Arnold Palmer, Julius Boros, and myself, drew the ball. You may say, "What about Ben Hogan?" Well, there I'll go with his old adversary Snead, who once said that he thought that Hogan was at his best when he let himself go off the tee and put a little draw on the ball.

One of the key adjustments all great players make as they get older is to use a stronger grip (both hands turned more to the right on the shaft) than when they were younger. When young, they all had very strong hand action, and as a consequence feared a hook. So they adopted a neutral or even a weak grip (both hands turned to the left on the shaft). With age, you don't have the strength to release the club as when younger. The stronger grip compensates for this, and also produces the desired draw.

Among the top seniors, Arnold Palmer has noticeably strengthened his grip in recent years. I, too, have recently made this adjustment. In fact, you won't see a successful senior player with a weak grip.

For amateurs, this grip adjustment is essential. Even if you were a straight ball hitter as a young player, you'll find the draw a good friend as you reach the senior ranks. If you were a fader or slicer, then you *must* learn to draw the ball.

To allow for the draw you'll produce with the stronger grip, you must, of course, aim and align your body right of target. You might not notice this adjustment with many senior players, who, like myself, only play for a slight draw. However, if you've watched Billy Casper hit a tee shot recently, it's immediately apparent, as Billy now hits a big hook, aiming very much to the right of target to allow for it. I should add: He's doing very well with it.

## THE YOUNG MAN'S SWING

BEFORE we get to my new "Walk-Through" swing, I think it's important to review the modern "Square-to-Square" swing. (See the following pages for illustrations of both.) This is because, as I've said, it's been so strongly "sold" in magazine articles, books, and on TV over the years—primarily, because the players featured are those winning on the PGA Tour. They're invariably young, strong, players, so every amateur thinks this is the only way to play. Once you have a clear picture of this "young man's swing," and why it's not for senior golfers, you can readily compare it with the "Walk-Through" swing and understand what changes you should make.

Overall, the "young man's swing" is a "big muscle" method: The strongest muscles in the body—the legs, hips, lower back and left latissimus dorsi (or "lat")—power the swing, driving the arms and club through the ball. It's a swing in which one coils the upper body strongly against the lower body going back, just like coiling a spring, then uncoils in the downswing. It's also a "closed to open" method, that is, one closes the clubface slightly or a lot (depending on one's strength) on the backswing, and works it back to a slightly open position in the follow-through—what's known as "blocking" the shot slightly. Now here's the swing in more detail.

To accommodate the strong leg drive laterally to the left in the downswing, the stance must be fairly wide—roughly shoulder width between the heels for a 5-iron and slightly wider with the longer clubs. For the same reason, one also needs to play the ball forward in the stance, about off the left heel with the driver, standing square to the ball, or even slightly open to further tighten the coil. The right foot is square to the target line, the left foot slightly turned out to the left. This also tightens the coil and, on the downswing, makes it

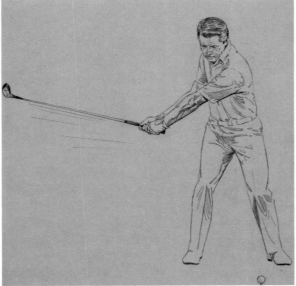

easier for the lower body to shift left and then turn out of the way. A neutral or a weak grip is used. The right leg is planted firmly, bracing it inward. The hands are fairly high—this keeps the hands "quiet" during the swing—in a "big muscle" swing, the hands are kept out of the swing as much as possible.

The takeaway is a one piece movement of the arms, shoulders, and club. As the club goes back, the idea is to "hold it down," that is, not allow it to open naturally. Rather, it should be kept slightly closed so that halfway back, where the clubshaft is horizontal to the ground, the clubface still partially faces the ground. As the shoulders continue to turn, the hips start their turn, but this movement is kept to a minimum. The right leg is kept braced inward, allowing little or no movement to the right. The upper body is turned around and against what is essentially a fixed right leg—a person could put a plank just outside the right side of the right leg at address and never touch it.

At the top of the swing, there has been a big shoulder turn, but little hip turn. The shoulders will have turned 90 to 120 degrees, the hips as little as 20 degrees. The left "lat" is stretched to its maximum. The left heel remains on the ground, or if pulled from the ground, only rises a little. The weight has shifted to the inside of the right foot. The left wrist is

"straight," in line with the left forearm, and the clubface is slightly closed (halfway between facing the sky and the toe pointing to the ground). With the strongest players, such as Arnold Palmer when he was younger, the wrist may even be slightly convex. Then the clubface is very closed, and will face the sky. This is the tightest "coil" one can make.

On the downswing, this pent-up energy is unleashed through the ball. The lower body unwinds, making a tremendous drive laterally to the left. Meanwhile, the upper body stays back as the arms and club are pulled down into the "late hit" position. As the hips start to clear, that is, turn to the left, the upper body continues to stay back or even moves farther to the right, and, while the wrists uncock, the club is worked from closed (at the top) to slightly open just after impact. The clubhead is driven straight down the line into a long, wide follow-through. In the finish, viewing the golfer from in front, there's a concave curve to the back—the so-called "reverse-C" position.

Such a swing demands strong hands, a strong body, and much flexibility. One must have strong hands that "own" the club at the top of the swing—any looseness in the hands spells disaster. One must be very flexible to turn the shoulders so much and the hips so little—allowing the left heel to rise too

much destroys the coil. Having a very strong back as well, and great flexibility to withstand the pressure of the legs driving forward on the downswing as the upper body stays back, are other requirements.

At a certain age, which varies according to individual fitness, you can't make this swing any more. In many cases, your hands aren't strong enough to hold on at the top. You've lost some flexibility. Your back won't stand the pressure. I've described it in detail so that you're aware of what it entails, but the fact is that I now feel so strongly about the subject, I wouldn't even teach a young man this swing any more, let alone a senior. I think it's outdated. If you persist in trying to execute it, you'll develop back problems, as I did. In short, you need another method.

## THE WALK-THROUGH SWING FOR SENIORS

WHEN I reached this stage myself, I did a lot of thinking, experimentation and research.

I realized that there never has been a great golfer who has lasted with a closed clubface. That "closed to open" swing must eventually injure his back. I noticed that the only golfers who did not have to change their swings as they got older were those like Christy O'Connor (affectionately called "Wristy Christy" by his peers), who has always used an "open to shut" type of swing. As Ben Hogan did before me, I found that open-

*Still the best way! Harry Vardon's cupped left wrist and open clubface.*

*No strain on the back here! Harry Vardon finishes forward, body erect.*

ing the blade, like the old Scottish pros, so that the left wrist was slightly cupped at the top, allowed me to hit hard with my whole body, just like a champion boxer delivering a knockout blow.

I also had the shining example of Sam Snead before me. Snead always allowed his hips to turn freely on the backswing. There was no effort to prevent the left heel from rising in the backswing, yet Snead had been one of the longest, straightest drivers in golf history. The same could be said of the immortal Bobby Jones, who achieved the Grand Slam of his day in 1930, winning the British and U.S. Opens and Amateurs.

The way the great golfers finished was also instructive. I saw that Hogan, Snead, Jones, Sarazen, and earlier greats like Harry Vardon, James Braid, and J.H. Taylor, never finished in a "re-verse-C" position. Rather, they released their backs in the follow-through so that they all finished well forward. Their weight was on the outside of the left heel, and the body was *erect*, even leaning a little toward the hole. They never suffered from back trouble, and I drew the obvious conclusion.

Why do I call the swing the "Walk-Through" swing? Because, in working on it, I often found that, on full swings, I was walking over my left foot in the finish with my right foot. This was caused by my complete transfer of weight to the left foot on the downswing. I was putting all my body weight into and through the ball, something which will only occur on swings where one uses full power, or from a slightly downhill lie.

One can trace the "Walk-Through" action back to the first winner of the British Open, one Willie Park, Sr., who took the championship four times. In 1896 his son Willie Park, Jr., wrote, "My father, who, it is well known, was one of the long-est, straightest drivers of his day, carried out the principle of the follow-through to such an extent that he used frequently to run a yard or two after his drive."

At any rate, it's clear that the "Walk-Through" swing has been used by the greatest champions over the years. It's just that it has become overlooked more recently because of the popularity of the "Square-to-Square" swing.

The "Walk-Through" action is something that used to dis-concert golf announcers on TV. They'd say something like, "Gary *completely* lost his balance on that one. He just kept on walking after the ball!" They thought I'd pushed the ball far to the right, but I hadn't, of course, and often they were forced to add that the ball finished close to the hole! I got a good chuckle when I heard of such stories after my rounds! Today, with my success using the swing, they seem to have accepted it. They'll simply say, "Here comes Gary with his 'Walk-Through' swing!"

Now let me give you the overall picture of the swing I want you to use.

At address, you should, of course, use the stronger grip and slightly closed stance, as stated above. However, the stance must also be narrower than when you were younger. If, as a senior, you use too wide a stance, the knees won't work properly. The left knee goes forward on the backswing, rather than behind the ball, as it should. Also, the right foot stays down too long coming through, and you're forced to come over the ball with the right shoulder. You swing from out to in, and slice.

You should modify your ball and foot position, too. Because your leg action isn't quite as strong as when younger, you'll need to play the ball slightly farther back in the stance toward the middle. You should no longer turn the left foot outward as much as when you were younger—it will restrict your backswing too much. Instead, turn it out only a little or even place it square to the target line if you've lost a lot of flexibility. I don't recommend turning out the right foot to the right, as is often recommended to seniors. Sure, you will be able to turn easier. However, too often this leads to a complete breakdown in the right leg on the backswing, and you sway to the right. Keep the right foot square to the line to help you wind up around a solid right leg.

Don't hold your hands too high at address. As I've said, this reduces hand action. If anything, carry them a little lower than

you did when younger. This will encourage the "open to shut" hand action we're looking for.

In the backswing, you'll still use a "one piece" takeaway. However, instead of just concentrating on the arms, club, and shoulders, include the left knee in the movement. As a young player, you never have to think of hip turn—your hips will turn enough just as a result of the shoulder turn. This is not true as a senior. To get a good shoulder turn, you need a good hip turn. You can't work on restricting the hip action, as you did when younger. Instead, emulate Snead: Allow your hips to turn and the left heel to rise enough so that you can get that good shoulder turn.

As you get older, you may not be able to keep the right leg as still on the backswing as you once could. Instead, you may have to allow the lower leg to become a shade more vertical than it was at address. You still shift the weight to the right foot going back, and wind up around a firm right leg. However, you'll probably have to give that right knee a little more freedom to get an adequate weight shift.

After the takeaway, you should let the left arm rotate to the right (clockwise) so that you open the clubface. This is a perfectly natural movement. However, you'll have to work on it if you've done the reverse, that is, holding down the club, for a long time. Halfway back, where the clubshaft is horizontal to

the ground, the clubface will have rotated slightly past the "straight ball" position, where the toe of the club points straight up at the sky. Instead, the clubface will have turned, say, another quarter inch or so more to the right—a slightly open position.

At the top of the swing, you'll have made a good shoulder turn of 90 degrees or so. Your hips will have turned about 45 degrees, and your left heel may well have been pulled a little from the ground, especially with the longer clubs. Your weight will have shifted to the flat of the right foot. One of the most important points is that the clubface must be open. The wrists will have cocked, with the left wrist slightly "cupped" and the toe of the club will point more or less to the ground.

On the forward swing, the action is very similar to throwing a ball. In fact, I tell all the golfers to whom I'm teaching the "Walk-Through" swing to throw a lot of balls underarm. It gives you the correct feeling of using the *whole body*, shifting your weight completely through the ball, just as you should in the swing. At impact, the upper body will be slightly more "over" the ball than in the "young man's swing," where the upper body is held back.

Also, since you rotated your left arm to the right going back, opening the clubface, you have to make a good release through impact, rotating the left arm to the left (counterclockwise).

This works the blade from open at the top to slightly closed at and after impact.

In the finish, you must at least be erect. As you start using the method, you'll find, as I did, that you won't necessarily walk through every time. However, the action is the same whether you do or not. You'll have put all your body weight into the ball, and in the follow-through, your body will at least be erect, and often leaning slightly toward the hole.

If a younger man or woman is reading this, he or she may do well to consider this. Although a good case can be made for the "Square-to-Square" swing being the ultimate power swing, the "Walk-Through" type of swing doesn't, as you can see, have too shabby a record! If you adopt it when younger, you'll never have to change your swing, and you'll never hurt your back!

In support of this, here's one more example. The name Henry Cotton may not mean much to you today here in the United States. However, in Europe the three-time British Open champion was revered both for his outstanding playing record and as a great teacher. In 1937, Cotton won his second British Open, leaving the pride of America—such players as Byron Nelson, Denny Shute, Henry Picard, Ed Dudley, Horton Smith, Sam Snead and Ralph Guldahl—trailing in his wake. In his prime, Cotton was one of the few golfers who could be mentioned as a supreme striker of the ball in the same breath as

Ben Hogan. Cotton *always* used an "open to shut" swing! Moreover, I vividly remember his demonstrating a 3-wood shot from a downhill lie in his book, *Study the Golf Game with Henry Cotton.* He said—and the sequence pictures showed him doing this—that the best way to play the shot was to "walk with the right leg down the hill in the finish....By letting the whole action flow in this way, *maximum power* [italics, mine] can be delivered with no fight against the pull of gravity."

Very interesting! Don't you agree?

Okay, then. That's the general idea of where we're headed on the swing. I know that most of you would like me to go immediately into how you acquire the "Walk-Through" swing. However, in all honesty it wouldn't be right. We must review the grip and address position first. As I said earlier, the type of swing you use is vitally important as you get older, but we can't work on that swing until we know that you have the static fundamentals down cold.

### *"Square-to-Square" swing—only for the young*

This swing demands great strength and flexibility. In the backswing, you tightly coil the upper body against the lower body. At the top, you've made a big shoulder turn, but little hip turn. The left wrist is "straight," the clubface closed, facing up. On the downswing, you unleash this energy through the ball, using tremendous leg drive and working the clubface from closed to open. The upper body stays back, resulting in a concave curve to the back in the finish, the "reverse C" position.

### *The "Walk-Through" swing for all seniors*

This type of swing gives you maximum power with no back strain. To draw the ball, you use a strong grip and a narrower, closed stance. Going back, the left arm rotates to the right. At the top the left wrist is "cupped," the clubface open, toe down. On the downswing, the action is like throwing a ball underarm. You close the clubface on the ball by shifting the weight of the whole body through the ball. You finish slightly leaning forward, and often you'll "walk through" the ball.

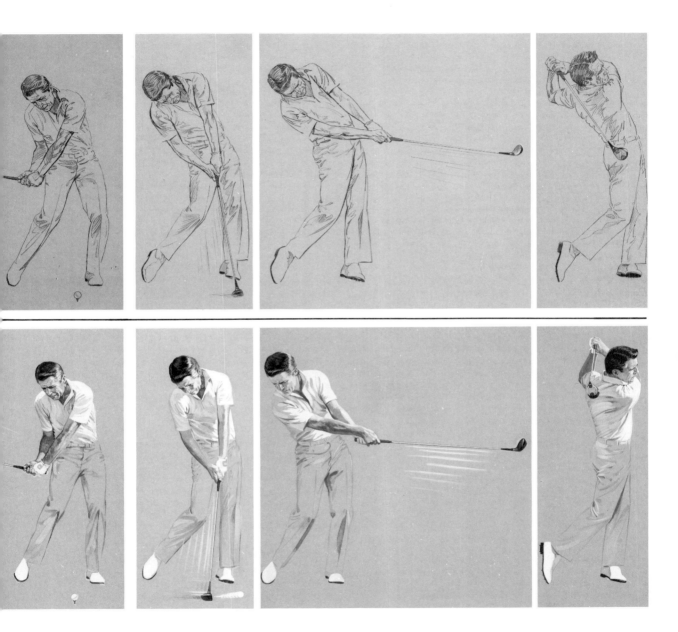

## CHAPTER TWO

# STRONGER IS BETTER

*Strong grip: Your grip should closely resemble ths one.*

*Weak grip: Avoid this grip except when you want to slice the ball.*

**B**EFORE WE GET TO THE MECHANICS of the correct grip, I want you to take a long, hard look at the illustrations labeled "strong grip" and "weak grip." If you're over fifty, your completed grip should closely resemble the illustration labeled "strong grip." You must avoid the one labeled "weak." Here's why.

The grip is much like the steering wheel of a car. Turning the whole grip to the right on the handle ("stronger") or left ("weaker") controls your hand action and the rotation of the arms to the left on the downswing, and thus the squaring of the blade at impact. Generally, the stronger the grip, the more the arms rotate to the left in the downswing, closing the clubface; the weaker the grip, the less rotation you get. With a very weak grip, the arms rotate slightly right in the downswing, opening the clubface.

Younger golfers as a rule have strong hands and forearms, and so they have a strong, fast rotation. If they adopt a very strong grip, they'll often hook their way right off the course. Some of them persist in using this grip, and manage to hit the ball fairly straight by dint of pulling the butt of the left hand through the ball—the ultimate "blocking" action. Even then, they'll let the left arm rotate once in a while and get a big snap hook. The smarter ones adopt a weaker grip so that they automatically hit the ball straight.

However, as you get older, the hands and arms tend to lose a little agility, and need some help in rotating the arms to the left through impact. Also, I'm suggesting that you learn to draw the ball, not just hit it straight. So, you definitely need a strong grip.

The first basic of the grip for seniors is that you should be able to see at least two knuckles of your left hand at address. If you still don't draw the ball, see *three*.

## TAKING THE GRIP

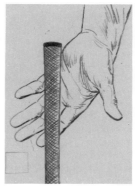

HOW you position the handle of the club in the hands is the second most important fundamental. You must get this right if you want to play up to your potential.

I've never seen a great golfer who has lasted with a poor grip, and seldom seen a poor player with a good grip. However, I have seen golfers who have a good grip, and not much else, who nevertheless manage to play pretty decent golf. That's how important a good grip is.

*The left hand grip is partially a palm, partially a finger grip.*

Put another way, if I had a sore throat, I'd go straight to my doctor. If I had a sore tooth, I'd go to my dentist. Yet, I've seen so many seniors who obviously have played bad golf for years. They've tried different swings, and often have spent a fortune on new clubs, but they never have taken a lesson from their PGA pro, who is their local "Doctor Golf." If they had, they would have learned that a poor grip was the root of most of their problems.

In the left hand, the grip is not entirely in the palm, yet not entirely in the fingers. The club should lie diagonally across the hand, from a point one-half inch below the first joint of the index finger to a point one-half inch above the root of the little finger. If your present grip is incorrect, a good tip is to mark these points on your glove with a pen until the correct position is ingrained.

You'll find that, when you close the hand, you can now hold the club securely, pinning the handle between the last three fingers of the hand underneath and the butt of the hand on top. Allow the left thumb to fall straight down the right side of the handle.

*You should be able to see three knuckles of the left hand.*

When taking the left hand grip, make sure that there is enough room at the top of the handle on which to place the butt of the hand. When you've completed the grip, you should be able to see at least one inch of handle above the little finger. Also, there should be no gap between the forefinger and thumb; this leads to looseness. To further secure the grip, *lightly* draw the thumb toward the index finger. This activates the large muscle at the base of the thumb and index finger.

*The right hand grip is in the fingers.*

The right hand grip is in the fingers. Initially, cradle the handle in the middle two fingers as shown, then fit the lifeline of the right palm snugly onto the left thumb. Maintain a light pressure between the two. The right thumb should be positioned on the left side of the handle.

As in the left hand, there must be no looseness, no gap between the index finger and thumb. Just as you did before, *lightly* draw the thumb toward the index finger so that the big muscle at their base is noticeable.

*In the completed grip, both palms should be parallel to each other.*

## PALMS PARALLEL

ANOTHER important grip fundamental is that the palm of the left hand must be parallel to that of the right. The hands must work together in the swing, not fight each other. They'll only do that if the palms are parallel.

Sadly, I often see seniors who have a strong left hand grip, while the right is very weak, very much turned to the left on top of the club. Another common mistake is a weak left hand and a strong right hand. These types of grip are fatal as the hands then work against each other during the swing and pull the body completely out of position. Not even Jack Nicklaus, Arnold Palmer, or myself for that matter, could play consistent golf with such a grip.

Here's a good little tip on this. From the completed grip with the club resting on the ground, extend the fingers of both hands. You can then easily see if the palms are parallel to each other. Periodically, check your grip this way.

Seniors: Remember—A tight grip reduces your flexibility and you'll lose distance. In the grip, "light" is right!

## GRIP PRESSURE

THE completed grip should feel unified, as though you had one big hand holding the club. However, I should emphasize that, especially for seniors, the grip pressure should not only be uniform but light, not tight.

I see so many seniors who grip the club far too tightly. Usually, this comes from a subconscious effort to get more distance, which in turn often stems from a desire to keep up with the youngsters!

A tight grip is invariably fatal, because it causes the *reverse* of what you want. Tension in the hands shortens the muscles in your hands and forearms and reduces the flexibility in your wrists. So, you end up with less distance, not more.

You must hold the club softly. Trust me—your grip pressure will tighten up automatically in response to the swing.

Equally well, of course, you must hold the club firmly enough so that you can control it. The grip can't be sloppy. This is especially true of the last three fingers of the left hand and the middle two of the right hand—these fingers must be firmly on the handle.

I wish I could give you a number, say, on a one to ten scale that would tell you how firm the grip pressure should be, but obviously I can't. First of all, we don't have such a scale, and second, the necessary grip pressure is to some extent individual, depending on such things as the strength of your fingers, the speed of your swing, and so on. However, here are a couple of tips that will help.

First, as you waggle the club before swinging, you should be able to feel the weight of the clubhead in your hands. If you can't, you're gripping too tightly. Your wrists must be free to hinge and unhinge. As Sam Snead said one time, your wrists should feel "oily" during the waggle.

Second, to test that your grip is firm enough, put one penny between the butt of your left hand and the top of the handle, and another between the lifeline of your right hand and the left thumb. Now take a swing. If either penny falls, then either your grip is incorrect—the handle is wrongly positioned in the hands—or it's too sloppy.

Another very good test for your grip—and the strength of your hands—is to hit three drives in succession without changing your grip. Have a friend tee the ball each time, and swing away. If your hands remain in position until the follow-through of that third drive, they and your grip are in very good shape.

## Overlap, Interlock, or Ten-Finger?

*The overlap or Vardon grip.*

I'VE left until last the question of the style of grip you adopt—overlap, interlock, or ten-finger (see illustrations). This is because the grip style is of very little importance compared to the correctness of your hold on the club. However, it does deserve a few words.

Generally, I recommend the overlap grip used by most of the golfers on the PGA Tour. However, if you don't "own" the club at the top, if it loosens, you might try the interlock, used by Jack Nicklaus and Tom Kite among others. The interlock can also feel more comfortable to people with fingers that are short in relation to the length of their palms.

It's worth noting that the normal interlock today finds the left thumb positioned down the right side of the handle, as in the overlap. However, Gene Sarazen and other earlier champions used a variation of the interlock, where the left thumb wrapped around the right side of the handle. This puts the handle more in the palm of the left hand. Usually this means that the grip must be built up, that is, made thicker, under the left hand to afford a secure grip. Although not used much today, the grip can be useful if you need thicker grips because of arthritis, or because an injury has made any degree of pressure on the left thumb unbearable.

---

**Super seniors: If arthritis makes the regular overlap grip painful, try the interlocking grip with the left thumb around the shaft. If you've lost a lot of power, try the ten-finger grip.**

*The modern interlock grip.*

*The ten finger grip.*

Super seniors (those over sixty years of age) often get to the stage where they lose a lot of distance. If this happens to you, you should realize that the ten-finger grip, with all the fingers on the club, can give you better hand action and thus more power than the other grips. It's also useful for those with small hands. Bob Rosburg and Art Wall are two older champions who use the grip. Today, it is seldom seen on the PGA Tour, although Dave Barr and Tim Norris are two golfers I can think of who use it successfully.

## CHAPTER THREE

# SET UP RIGHT

THE OLD CHINESE PROVERB says it best: One picture is worth more than 10,000 words. Before you read on about the detail of the correct address, I would like you to take a good look at the next illustrations that appear on page 45. Notice two things: 1. With the driver and 5-iron, I've taken a closed stance, my body lined up to the right of the target. 2. The ball is farther back in the stance than is commonly taught.

The reason, of course, why I've taken a closed stance is to allow for the draw I want you all to acquire. However, the reason why the ball is back in the stance is not only because, as a senior, your leg action is not as strong as it once was. There's a second reason: Ball position and body alignment work together. You must understand that if you're going to learn to draw the ball.

When I came into the Masters in 1978, I was doing something that was uncharacteristic of my game—I was fading the ball. I realized that I was in trouble, because at Augusta you've got to hit practically every shot with a draw! Then my son Wayne said to me, "Put the ball back in your stance." Immediately, I saw my mistake. Without noticing it, I had positioned the ball too far forward in my stance, and this had slightly opened up my feet and shoulders. With that setup, I then swung a little from out to in across the ball, creating the fade!

As soon as I put the ball farther back, I could draw the ball, and I went on to win my third green jacket.

There are two morals to the story. First, of course, the farther forward you play the ball, the more you tend to open the stance; the farther back, the more you tend to close it. However, second, and equally important, it's the little details of address that can often make the difference. It doesn't matter how experienced you are, you must continually check every facet of your address position. As I've said, most "swing faults" actually come from a poor address.

Now, a good address position doesn't guarantee a good swing. However, it does give you the best chance to start and complete the swing correctly. I usually can tell the handicap of a player within a few strokes just by looking at him set up. If you look like a good golfer at address, you'll probably swing well, too.

The opposite is also true. A faulty address will lead to a faulty backswing, and, unless you have the ability to compensate for it, it will lead to a poor downswing. It's worth pointing out that, the older you get, the more your reflexes slow down and the more difficult it becomes to make such compensations with the club in motion.

All professionals know this. This is why at every Senior Tour stop, you'll see us practicing with clubs laid on the ground to help verify such points as correct alignment, ball position, and so on. I urge every senior to do the same.

## IMPACT SHAPES YOUR ADDRESS

ONE of the best statements I've ever heard about the address was made by Australian Peter Thomson, the five-time British Open champion. He said that the best way to set up in a good address position is to think of the position you want your body to be in at impact and go from there. I couldn't agree more.

At impact, you want your feet and shoulders square to your intended line of swing. You want your left arm extended in line with the club shaft, your right arm bent, your lower body weight on the left foot. Your upper body, and certainly your head should be behind the ball so that you can hit the ball forward.

---

**Seniors: A poor address position creates a poor swing—unless you can compensate for it during the swing. The older you get, the harder it is to do this, because the reflexes slow down. With a good address, you don't have to compensate!**

A good address faithfully mirrors the above. The only exception is that the weight is equally distributed between the feet. However, as we'll see later, the forward press not only gets the swing started smoothly, it also puts the weight momentarily on the left foot.

## THE ADDRESS, FROM TOES TO TOP

FOR a senior, I'd recommend never to spread the feet wider than the width of the shoulders, measured from between the heels. I know you may have heard this before, but I feel I have to repeat it, because there seem to be a lot of Texans out there who feel their shoulders are three feet wide!

For a driver, place the feet about shoulder width apart. This places the upper body sufficiently behind the ball so that you can deliver a good sweeping blow. Progressively narrow the stance as you go down the set to the more lofted clubs. This puts the upper body slightly more "over" the ball, programming a slightly descending blow.

A good tip is periodically to take your stance, say, with a driver, then let go of the club and let your arms hang down. If you extend each forefinger in turn, you can get a good idea whether your heels are no more than shoulder width apart.

On all full shots with woods and irons, set up the desired draw by adopting a slightly closed stance, aligning the feet and shoulders slightly right of target. The only time you use an open stance, with the feet and shoulders aligned to the left of target, is when you want some slice spin, such as on bunker shots and pitch shots with the wedges.

Do guard against playing the ball too far forward in the stance. As a rough guide, play the driver no farther forward than about two inches inside the left heel. Then as you go down to the short irons, put the ball slightly farther back in the stance. You then catch the ball a little earlier in the downswing

Seniors: Watch out for "Seniors' slump." Late in the round, fatigue can lead to poor posture—and bad swings.

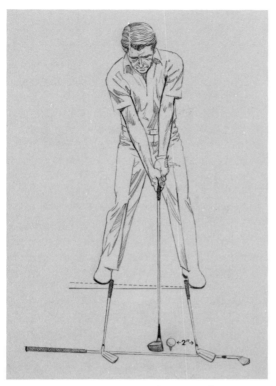

With the driver use a closed stance, the feet shoulder width apart.

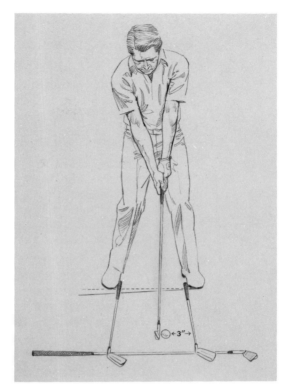

With a 5-iron, use a closed, slightly narrower stance, ball slightly back.

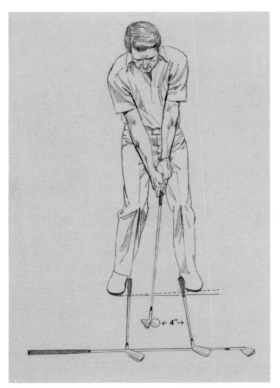

With a wedge, you usually want to cut the ball. So, use an open stance.

Lean forward from the hips, with the knees flexed, the back straight.

arc, while the clubhead is still descending. In this way, you take a divot after the ball and put the desired backspin on it. For a 5-iron, position the ball about an inch farther back toward the middle of the stance from the driver position, and for a wedge about an inch farther back than the 5-iron.

Seniors should also check their posture frequently, especially late in the round, when fatigue can creep in and you can get to slumping over the ball. You want to stand tall, then lean forward from the hips, keeping the back straight and allowing the arms to hang from the shoulders. Because your right hand is lower on the club than the left, the left shoulder should be slightly higher than the right. Your left side and arm should feel slightly stretched while the whole right side should be relaxed, the right arm slightly "inside" the left, that is, closer to the side. There should be a light pressure of the upper left arm against the left pectoral muscle. This, as we'll see in the next chapter, is what helps you swing on plane.

I've found that many seniors tend to set up with the shoulders level and the right arm too straight and thrust away from the side. This opens the shoulders, and sets up an out-to-in swing, and a slice. A good little tip here is take off your right shoe and then address a ball. This gives you the feel of the correct shoulder and arm position very quickly. You can also test whether you're correct with the aid of a friend standing to your right. If you're in the correct position, the friend should be able to insert the shaft of a club horizontally between your arms so that the shaft touches the back of the left arm at the elbow and the inside of the right elbow.

A very important point for seniors is that the knees should be slightly flexed so that you lower the derriere into a slight "sit down" position. As a class, seniors don't flex their knees enough, which makes for a "dead-legged" arm swing. You should feel solidly grounded, the weight equally divided between the feet and between the heels and balls of the feet. The knees should also be flexed slightly inward, toward each other. Then, they'll perform properly during the swing.

The left knee should break behind the ball going back, while the right leg remains firm. On the forward swing, the right knee should move to the left into the follow-through. Setting the knees a little "inward" sets up these correct actions.

A very good test of your posture is to take your address, and then have a friend try to push you off balance. If you wobble, then adjust your knee flex and weight distribution until all that happens is that the legs just firm up to resist the pressure.

> **Seniors: As the old-time Austrian ski instructors used to say, "Benden die knees!" Stiff legs lead to loss of power.**

To adjust to the different lengths and lies of the various clubs, simply alter the arm and hand position and the distance of your body from the ball. With the driver, the longest club in the bag, you measure to the ball with your extended left arm and the hands and arms must be a little farther from the body. As the clubs become shorter and the lie more upright, you stand closer to the ball, with the hands and arms closer to the body.

## THE ADDRESS STEP BY STEP

WHEN you've watched tour professionals play, no doubt you've been impressed by the meticulous way they take their address position. Each player has his own individual step-by-step procedure, which is repeated exactly before every stroke. You should do the same. A repetitive procedure for taking address, also known as a "routine" or "pattern," breeds consistency, an important goal for every senior.

For most people, the procedure begins immediately after you've taken the club out of the bag. From there go behind the ball, looking toward the target. Starting from this position allows you to get a clear picture of your target and visualize the swing and trajectory of the shot you want to make. It also allows you to identify your intended line of swing, so that you can square your clubhead and body to the line.

It's worth pointing out that, if something disturbs your concentration in the middle of your procedure, never, but never, try to pick it up from that point. You'll invariably upset the pattern and miss the shot. This thought applies to every shot in the bag, from the driver to the putter. Instead, start your procedure over again from the beginning. Then, you can put the distraction behind you and, with a fresh start, you'll play a successful shot.

On the Senior Tour, Billy Casper is a marvellous illustration of this principle. His procedure starts from the moment he takes his club from his bag. If he gets disturbed, he'll actually put the club back in the bag, and begin again from there!

It's also worth pointing out that starting from directly behind the ball helps you set up with a square stance. However, if you want to draw the ball, as we seniors should do on all normal full shots, you must align your feet and shoulders slightly right of target. In that case, you'll find it helpful to start from a position slightly left of a position directly behind the ball. Conversely, when you want to cut the ball, start slightly right of directly behind the ball.

The next steps are to walk to the side of the ball, sole the club behind the ball, take your grip, and, assuming you're drawing the ball, aim the clubface squarely to a point slightly right of target. Then spread your feet into the correct stance.

Here I'd like to interject that many seniors apparently find it difficult to position the ball in the correct position in the stance consistently. If you're one of them, I suggest you aim the club with your feet together and the ball centered between the feet. It then becomes easy first to move the left foot to the left and place the ball in the correct position relative to it, then move the right foot to the right into the correct stance width and alignment.

Once you've taken your address, you must keep in motion as you take your final looks at the intended line of swing and your target. Shift your weight slightly from one foot to the other as you finalize your address. Another aid to keeping in motion is to waggle the club. Perhaps the best is a one piece back and forth movement with no wrist break. Byron Nelson did this, and it's helpful because it previews the correct one piece takeaway. If that doesn't work for you, then waggle, like Sam Snead, with a full wrist break. What you personally do I'll leave to your individual taste, just as long as you obey the greatest commandment of the pre-shot procedure, "Thou shalt not freeze!" Remember: The whole purpose of the procedure is to let you set up correctly and go so smoothly into your swing that no excess tension can creep in. That purpose is totally defeated if, like many seniors with whom I've played, you freeze at address and stare at the ball for what can seem like minutes to the impatient onlooker!

---

**Seniors: Don't "freeze" over the ball—this kills your freedom of swing. Stay in motion from the time you take your club out of the bag to the moment you start your backswing.**

Talking about looking at the ball reminds me that, rather than just look at the whole ball, I've found it very helpful to look at a particular spot on the ball, depending on the type of shot I want to hit. For example, if you want a "sweeping" hit, look at the back of the ball. On a driver, you can tee up the ball with the name of the ball at the back right at the equator, a useful aid. On the other hand, where you want a downward blow, as with irons, fix your eyes on the top of the ball, and try to hit down on that spot.

The last action before the swing is what is called the "forward press." I like my own here, of course. I move my right knee inward and shift a little weight to the left foot. This gives me a preview of the correct impact position, where the weight should be on the left foot. From there, I can shift my weight smoothly to my right foot in the takeaway. It's much easier to make this forward-and-back move than try to start the backswing from a dead stop.

However, one can't be too dogmatic about the type of forward press to use. Jack Nicklaus, for example, prefers not to ground his club behind the ball; he just lets it hang from his shoulders, hovering it just above the ground behind the ball. His last move before the swing is to turn his head to the right as he firms up his left side.

Actually, any little move is good, provided it leads you smoothly into the takeaway.

One final thought before we go to the mechanics of the swing. Many back problems can come, not just from a "reverse-C" type of swing, but simply from years of teeing up the ball incorrectly. If you lean over with stiff legs to tee the ball—or for that matter to take it out of the hole—you're asking for trouble. Your knees were made to bend.

*CHAPTER FOUR*

# *LEARNING THE WALK-THROUGH SWING*

A S A YOUNG MAN, I was convinced that the way I swung the club was the correct way. As I got a little older, and was exposed to all the great players, I started to wonder.

I saw Sam Snead, who took the club very much inside the line, then up to the top. Bob Jones did the same, and today Ray Floyd does it, too. Byron Nelson took the club back with no wrist break, and only fully cocked the wrists on the downswing. Today, Johnny Miller cocks his wrists early and retains his wrist cock until the hit. Miller Barber takes the club back very much outside the line, closing the blade, then loops it back to the inside and to a square position at impact. Don January takes the longest swing imaginable, while Doug Sanders takes such a short one, we still tease him out on the Senior Tour, saying that he's the only golfer alive who can hit a drive from a telephone booth!

Now that I have the perspective of a man of fifty-plus, I'm convinced that, while there obviously isn't just one way to swing effectively, there certainly is *one easiest, most reliable way to swing.* Granted, it does appear as though all you have to do is to get the downswing right. Despite their assorted backswings, all the great players manage to deliver the club to the ball the same way: They come down from the inside, hit late, have the weight on the left foot at impact, the left arm is straight, the right arm is bent, and so on. However, to do it, many have to reroute the club onto the correct downswing plane. I'm convinced that if your backswing is on plane, as Hogan's was and mine is, it's far easier to stay on plane in the downswing, far easier to consistently deliver a solid blow.

You have to remember that all the great golfers practice and play golf practically every day. Even on travel days, most tour pros will at least hit a few balls. In conversation, they'll only bring up the days they *didn't* play golf. In contrast, the average senior tells you the days he or she *did* play golf—in most cases only one or two days a week.

That's why you need the most reliable method going, one where no compensations are needed, one that demands the least amount of practice, one so simple that you can work on it when you're at home with just a minimum of equipment. In the swing I'm going to teach you—the "Walk-Through" swing —you not only avoid any possibility of hurting your back, you also stay on plane all the way. So it's sound for seniors as well as safe.

## THE SWING PLANE

BEFORE we go further, I should explain what I mean by swing plane. In fact, swing plane is basically a very simple concept. We swing the club in a circular arc, which is at an angle to the ground. If we could hit the ball from between our feet (patently impossible, of course), we could then use a perfectly upright swing plane like one of the big Ferris wheels at a fairground. If we had to hit every ball, say, from a chest-high position in a bush, then we would have to swing on a horizontal plane, like a carousel or merry-go-round. However, in golf, the ball is on the ground, so our swing plane must be about half way between vertical and horizontal.

To check whether your own swing is on plane, you need to know just this one rule: To be on plane, your clubshaft must either be *parallel* to the intended swing line at certain moments, or *point directly at it* at others. If the club is in any other position at any point in the swing, it is off plane.

## PRACTICE THE RIGHT POSITIONS

To acquire the "Walk-Through" swing, you should first ingrain the seven key swing positions illustrated in Chapter One and repeated on the following pages. Get these positions correct, and not only will your whole swing be on plane, it will be fundamentally correct. I'll tell you how to practice the positions in a moment, but first I'd like to impress on you the importance of precision. Practicing these positions feeds them into your muscle memory, like feeding data into a computer.

Feed in the correct positions and your swing will improve, but feed in incorrect positions, and you actually ingrain bad moves. As they say in the computer business—Garbage In, Garbage Out (GIGO). So, study the details of the positions, and when you're practicing them, check everything—your club-face, your hands, wrists, arms, legs, hips, and shoulders—against the illustrations and descriptions in the text so that you get everything correct. I should note that in positions 2,3,4,5, and 6, the clubface positions are those for a draw, the shape of shot I want you to acquire. Here are the seven positions in brief.

**1. Address,** where the feet and shoulders are set up on a line parallel to the intended line of swing. The clubshaft points at the line.

**2. Halfway back,** where the club is horizontal to the ground. This is the first position where the clubshaft be-

Position 1.
*Address*

Position 2.
*Halfway back*

comes parallel to the swing line. The left arm has rotated the club to the right just past a "toe up" position, the "straight ball" position, so that it points a little behind the player. The clubface is very slightly facing up.

**3. Top of the swing,** where the clubshaft is horizontal to the ground and again parallel to the swing line. The weight has shifted to the right foot. The toe of the club points down.

**4. Halfway down,** where the shaft is horizontal to the ground, and again parallel to the swing line. The toe of the club points upward and just a little behind the player.

**5. Impact,** where the weight is on the left foot, the left arm is straight, the right arm is bent, and the clubshaft points at the line. The clubface will be a little closed.

*Position 3.*
*Top of swing*

*Position 4.*
*Halfway down*

*Position 5*
*Impact*

**6. Halfway through** into the follow-through, where again the shaft is horizontal to the ground and parallel to the swing line. The left arm has rotated the club to the left just past the "straight ball" position, where the toe would point straight up. The toe of the club points upward, but also a little behind the player, the clubface facing just a little downward.

**7. Finish,** where all the weight is on the outside of the left heel, the body is leaning a little forward and faces left of the target, and the club has swung behind the back, the shaft pointing at the line.

*Position 6.*
*Halfway through*

*Position 7.*
*Finish*

## USE A HEAVY CLUB

TO ingrain these positions, you need to acquire a heavy club. You'll find that, with the heavy club, you'll perfect them far faster than with a club of normal weight. You can ask your pro to get you one of the heavy drivers available commercially or make up your own heavy club from an old, stiff-shafted driver and add extra weight to it.

*However, do make certain that, whatever you use, it's not too heavy for you. Remember the golden rule of any weight work: Start with a lighter weight, then as you get stronger, add additional weight.*

Set up a full length mirror at home, and pose in each of these positions for a few seconds at a time. A good plan is fill the "spaces" between the positions by swinging in ultra-slow motion. Address the ball with the club slightly off the ground, hold it for a few seconds, swing slowly to the second position, hold it, and so on. Work up to about five repetitions a day, and you'll speedily make progress.

After you've done your positions, then make some full swings, also in slow motion. *Swing at the speed you can comfortably make, which, with a heavy club, is sure to be a lot slower than your normal swing speed. You can hurt yourself if you try to swing too fast.* You'll find that one beauty of the heavy club is this: If you start the swing in the right way, slightly inside and in one piece, it becomes extremely difficult to make off-plane moves! Start by taking, say, five swings with the heavy club, then gradually work up to swinging it for five or even ten minutes a day. From day to day, listen to your muscles; when they start to complain, quit.

If you don't have much headroom in your home, then try using a sand wedge to which you've attached one or two "donut-shape" weights, which are also easily obtainable.

## GET ON THE BOARD

ANOTHER great aid to swinging on plane is what I call the "board." This is simply a plank of wood that you position just outside the ball, parallel to the line of swing (see illustrations on pages 56-57). To swing on plane, your clubhead must stay "inside" the board all the way.

You can set up a board in your home for your position and slow-motion work with the heavy club. However, I also like to use the board on the practice ground. Then you can combine position work, slow-motion swings, and actual hitting of balls. In fact, I often do this when I'm at home. If you get a plank of wood at least two inches wide—say a "two by eight," about four feet long—it will stand up on edge by itself.

If I'm on the road and don't have a board handy, what I'll

often do is ask the local professional if I might have a box in which new clubs are delivered. This makes an excellent substitute. If that's not possible, then I'll use an arrangement of three clubs on the ground in practice: I place the first one parallel to the swing line just outside the ball, the second parallel to the first across my toes, and, to check on ball position, a third one across and at right angles to the second club. This third club would extend up to a point some six inches from the ball.

Set up with your feet and shoulders parallel to the board, as I'm doing in the illustrations. I'm using a 5-iron here, and so am drawing the ball. That's why the whole swing plane, and therefore the board as well, is set slightly right of the ultimate target. In other words, I swing back slightly inside the board to the top, where the shaft is parallel to the board. Then, I'll swing through parallel to the board, starting the ball right of the target. However, the strong grip I'm using will slightly close the blade at impact, so that the ball will eventually draw back to the target.

The board will speedily reveal off-plane swings. The most common ones I see among seniors are, as you might imagine,

of the "out to in" type, which produce a slice (see illustrations on pages 58–59). If you take the club back outside the board, as shown, in the first illustration, you'll swing the club up into a "laid off" position at the top (the club shaft points behind you as in the second illustration), come down from out to in, and you're very likely to hit the board before impact, known as "coming over the top" (third illustration). However, it's equally possible to take the club inside too much, "cross the line" at the top (the club points slightly in front of you), and come through too much from in to out. Do this and you'll strike the board after impact.

Of the two positions at the top—"laid off" and "crossing the line"—I'd much prefer to see you slightly crossing the line. At least, you'll still be drawing the ball, a strong shot. Avoid the laid off position like the plague; it usually leads to a slice. As Gardner Dickinson, a great teacher, once told me, "I've never seen a senior who plays well laying off."

Hitting the board provides a strong deterrent to off-plane motions. You're almost forced to swing correctly.

A very useful aid, when practicing outdoors with the board, is do it with a friend. Take along a Polaroid camera, and snap

**Right:** Set up the board parallel to the intended line of swing. Your clubhead must always stay inside the board. Note the takeaway is to the inside. At the top, the clubshaft is parallel to the board. Swing through parallel to board.

enough pictures of each other so that you can check that all your key positions are correct and you're swinging on plane.

Now, I'd like to zero in on other important details of the swing that you should work on.

## WIDE TO NARROW

THE correct takeaway, which I define as the first two feet of the backswing, is essential. Previously, you'll remember I talked of a "one piece" takeaway. I've demonstrated the correct method in the accompanying photos of address and takeaway. Note that I haven't cocked my wrists at all, I haven't turned the left arm to the left (or right), that I'm taking the arms and club back with the shoulder turn and allowing the left knee to work slightly forward and to the right. All this is happening in one move. That's "one piece."

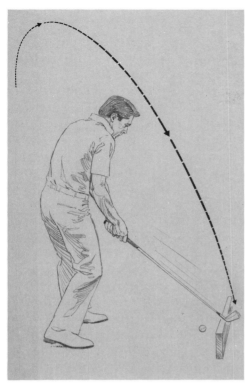

***Wrong:*** Here's the typical slicer's swing. The takeaway goes outside the board. At the top, the player has lifted the club with hs arms into a "laid off" position. He then swings down from out to in, cutting across the ball.

*For the first two feet of the takeaway, take the club back in one piece, the arms, shoulders, left knee, hands, and club working together.*

**Seniors: Watch out for the "lazy man's" turn. If you don't feel a little tension in the left side of your back at the top of the swing, you've probably "cheated" on your body turn. You're probably lifting your arms instead of turning your hips and shoulders.**

The one piece takeaway does a lot for you. First, it gets the whole body moving together in a coordinated fashion. The weight shift, the windup around the right leg, the hip turn, the shoulder turn, all have been set in motion.

Second, and very important, it sets up *width* in the backswing. Now, you may not be able to make as wide a backswing as you used to, but every normal backswing must have width. This is because of Newton's Law, "To every action, there is an equal and opposite reaction."

If you have a wide backswing, then you'll tend to react by swinging down in a narrow arc, pulling the club down into the "late hit" position, and hitting with maximum force. The most powerful golf swings are always "wide to narrow."

However, if you break the wrists off the ball, you're very likely to "lift" the club with your arms above the plane, bend your left arm (narrow) and never make a good body turn. On the downswing, you'll react by coming down "wide," throwing the club from the top of the swing, that is, uncocking the wrists too soon. You'll not only lose power, you'll probably come across the ball from out to in and slice it.

Yes, I know that Johnny Miller and Hubert Green break their wrists off the ball. They're very talented exceptions to the rule. They break their wrists while still getting a good turn. However, most seniors would merely "lift," "bend," and then "throw."

So, take the club back in one piece. Then, and only then, allow the left arm to rotate to the right.

## THE ON-PLANE BACKSWING

PLEASE look for a moment at the photo of me at the top of the swing. Note especially the position of the left arm—it has swung across the chest and has "cut" across the tip of the right shoulder. If your posture was good at address and you make

*At the top of the swing, the left arm should intersect the right shoulder.*

this move, then you are on plane at the top. That's a very important checkpoint.

Don't let appearances deceive you. A taller golfer like a Johnny Miller will lean over the ball a little more than I do. However, he will make exactly the same move in the backswing and his left arm will be in exactly the same position in relation to the right shoulder as mine is. In other words, what's making the plane of the swing a little more upright is the slightly increased forward lean at address, not a different golf swing.

What I want you to avoid is any "lifting" of the arm on the backswing. Jack Nicklaus, I know, did this, when younger, and it can be a powerful move if you have the same physical equipment as Jack had when he was a young man—huge, immensely powerful legs. I remember Arnold Palmer saying one time, "If that young man [Jack Nicklaus] didn't have legs like Atlas, he would be in trouble!" And he was right! Nicklaus' legs were strong enough to pull the club down to the inside so that Jack met the ball powerfully. However, most seniors using the "flying right elbow" won't have the strength in the legs to reroute the club back to the inside on the downswing. Instead, they'll come "over the top" and hack across the ball.

In more recent years, a slimmer and slightly less powerful Nicklaus has gone to what seems like a flatter swing, but in fact it's one where the left arm, instead of "lifting," now works as I have described. As a result, the right arm no longer "flies" —it stays a lot closer to the body and under control

As I said earlier, the key to swinging on plane on the backswing is to press the upper left arm lightly against the left pectoral muscle. If you just maintain that pressure during the backswing, you'll land up in the right position at the top. It's that simple.

## Swing Slow, Swing Full

AS Don January once told me, "Slow is long, fast is short." There's a wealth of wisdom in that remark.

At the top of the swing, you want a wide backswing, one with a full shoulder turn and as much hip turn as is necessary for you to make that good shoulder turn. You want to have wound up around a firm right leg. You want your weight on the right foot, in position to be moved through the ball. You want your left arm to have swung across the chest, and the wrists to have cocked. All this takes time.

If you rush the backswing, you never wind up correctly. In order to "save" the shot, you're then forced to try to get power the wrong way—by an "early hit" or an "over the top" move. Many seniors make this mistake.

Actually, I've already given you one of the secrets to swinging back more slowly, and that is the "one piece" takeaway. By getting the big muscles of the legs, hips, back, and shoulders moving immediately, it's almost impossible to take the club away too fast. These big muscles simply can't move as quickly as the smaller ones of the hands and wrists. However, it's possible for you to get the takeaway correct, and still cut off the backswing before it's completed, just by getting a little anxious.

So, give yourself the time to complete the backswing. As the older golfers used to say, "Wait for it." What "it" is will depend on what you're working on at the moment—it could be waiting to feel some pressure in the right heel before starting down, or the weight of the clubhead in the hands as the wrists com-

---

**Seniors: Never rush your backswing—you'll be forced to hit early and lose power. Remember what the old Scottish pros used to say: "You don't hit the ball with your backswing, laddie!"**

> **Seniors: If you tend to hit too early, first make a good solid turn, then "pull down on the bell rope."**

plete their cocking—but whatever "it" is, a complete backswing is well worth the wait. It puts you in the best position to make a smooth transition from backswing to downswing and get the desired "late hit."

Another reason why "slower is better" for seniors is that, with age, many seniors do lose some strength, although I'll show you how to hang on to as much of it as possible in the second part of this book. If you swing too fast, you may not have the strength to hold onto the club at the top of the swing.

As Tommy Bolt once said to me, "Son, you've got to 'own' the club at the top." You can't "own" it if you swing too fast!

Whenever I get to swinging too fast, I'll say to myself, "Swing fast and you'll never last, but swing slow, and you'll make the dough." Try it. It works for me.

## Pull Down to Hit Late

THERE'S no doubt in my mind that the single most important thing for seniors to practice is getting into the "late hit zone." What you have to do is learn to "pull down" from the top. (Please refer to the photos on page 64.) When you do this, you come down "narrow," in position to generate tremendous centrifugal force through the ball.

The correct first move down is the unwinding of the right leg, which drives to the left, shifting the weight to the left foot. The hips also unwind and the upper body is pulled down, the arms and club dropping to waist level, retaining the same shape they were in at the top. In fact, there may be a little increased cocking of the wrists. The right elbow goes into the side.

At this point centrifugal force should take over, and, as the hips continue to turn to the left, the upper body, arms, and then the club are released forcefully through the ball.

In my own best swings, I'll feel the first move down, and then not much else other than the outward tug of the centrifugal force as the body and club flash through. It's all over so quickly. The next thing I'm doing is following through and watching the flight of the ball. This is as it should be. A good golfer trusts centrifugal force to do the job for him.

However, with many seniors, a good backswing is no guarantee of a good downswing. For some reason, the lower part of the body doesn't work as well as when you were younger. All too often, you can still get too early a hit, a throwing of the club from the top, or an "over the top" move with the right shoulder. When you hit too early, your weight stays back on the right foot, and you get no leverage.

The obvious solution, of course, is to use some lower body key like "drive the right leg to the left," "drive the hips left," "turn the hips left," and so on. However, when you key on just the lower body, I've found that usually you'll overdo it and get the whole action out of sync.

I've talked extensively about this problem with Sam Snead and Chi Chi Rodriguez, two seniors who both use the "Walk-Through" type of swing. We all agreed that the best key we'd found is: *Imagine you are holding a bell rope and are pulling down on it.* This image coordinates the action of the lower and upper body so that everything stays in sync. Also, when you pull down inside, your right shoulder goes down and under the head, you delay the clubhead correctly, make a full shift of

*The right leg unwinds first, driving to the left. This unwinds the hips and then the upper body, pulling down the arms and club for the late hit.*

weight to the left giving maximum leverage, and release the back in the finish. In short, you get the right type of down-swing.

However, for most senior amateurs, this "pull down on the rope" key only works after they've experienced the correct movement—in many cases, they've been hitting early all their golfing lives. What you'll need are the following drills that make you perform the correct action. Then, you can build up the correct feel, and then you can use the "pull down on the rope" key to trigger the move during the swing.

**The "Buddy" Drill.** I was with my friend Bruce Rappaport in Geneva one time. Bruce, a businessman who has sponsored a pro-am every year for the last thirty years or so in Geneva to the tune of some four or five hundred thousand dollars, was "catching fish" from the top—that is, casting and throwing the club away. I told him about the "pull down on the rope" key,

*To learn the "pull down" action, have a friend hold the shaft as you make your first move down.*

*To work on the "late hit," grip with the right hand below the left, swing to the top, then pull down with the left side while resisting with the right arm.*

but he still continued to hit too early much of the time. So, I had him swing to the top, stop, and I held onto the club as he made his first move down (as a friend is doing for me in the photo). My holding onto the club forced him to "pull down on the rope." From the photo, you can see that my legs and hips have moved left and that I'm in a very good "pull down" position.

I remember that Bruce went from a poor twenty-three handicapper to a good eighteen just from learning this move. Try this drill with a friend. It conveys the feel of the correct movement far faster than words.

**"Hands Separated" Drill.** If you're by yourself, here's another drill that conveys the correct feel. In this case, you have to work one set of muscles against another. Take your address as shown, with the right hand well below the left. Go back to the top of the swing and pause for a moment. Now pull down on "the rope" with the left arm, left side, and the legs while you resist with the right arm. As you can see from the photos, this gives you excellent "pull down" and "halfway down" positions.

# THE RELEASE

REMEMBER: You opened the club going back, and after the "pull down" the clubface is still open; at the "halfway down" position, the toe of the club still points skyward and a little behind you. Yet, by the "halfway through" position the clubface is closed, the toe again pointing up and a little behind you. There has to be an action in between these positions that will slightly close the clubface by the time you meet the ball. There is: It's called the release.

The release really has two main components: 1. Rotating the left arm to the left from hip high in the downswing to hip high in the follow-through and letting the wrists uncock; 2. Rotating the whole body to the left while you're shifting the weight through, the "Walk-Through" action.

While it's true that in a good golfer's swing the whole release will occur spontaneously—as I said, all the good golfer does is get the first "pull down" move going and the rest just happens —it doesn't necessarily occur with senior amateurs.

There are several reasons for this. First, as you'll see later, if you're a slicer, you don't release properly. Second, it can be due to your *persisting with too weak* a grip or with other remnants of the "reverse-C" swing such as closing the clubface on the backswing. Third, even if you're correct at the "pull down" position, you could be interfering with the centrifugal force action. *In other words, you simply don't let it take over control of the swing, which is what you should do.* This is because you may well have the wrong idea of what you're trying to do on the downswing.

If you think you must apply the club to the ball, or try to steer the ball to the target, you'll kill the centrifugal force. All you'll succeed in doing is to slow the club down and take it off plane. You'll also never release. If you've worked along with my instructions so far, and you're still hitting the ball with a fade or slice, that's the problem. As we tour professionals say, you're "blocking" the shot.

Here's an excellent drill that overcomes this and other problems.

**Feet Together Drill.** Put your feet close together, about six inches apart is good, and hit some shots as I am doing in the accompanying photos. After many years of practicing this drill, I can do it with a driver. However, for a start, I suggest you use a well lofted club like a 5- or 7-iron before graduating

*The "feet together" drill teaches you strong hand action.*

to longer clubs. Also, tee up the ball slightly for further confidence.

You'll find that, because the "feet together" drill takes the legs out of the swing to a large extent, you're forced to make the swing mainly with the hands and arms. If you open the clubface going back, then the correct rotation of the left arm coming through the ball will occur very naturally. You'll start using crisp hand action through the ball, just like the pros— perhaps for the first time in your life.

The drill also prevents you from swinging too fast or making jerky movements. Do either and you'll lose your balance. Only a smooth, swinging action of the club will do.

If you have difficulty with the drill, then check the following points.

If there's no crispness, chances are you're still gripping too tightly. With too tight a grip, the wrists can't cock and uncock freely.

If you're still slicing, then hit the ball for a while with just a half-swing back and through. Swing back to position 2 and through to position 6, and check the position of your clubface in position 6. You'll find that instead of the toe of the club pointing upward and a little behind you, a slightly closed position, the *face* of the club is facing upward, an open position. This shows that instead of rotating the left arm and club to the left through the ball, you have a reverse rotation to the right— you're "blocking" the shot. Very probably, you're still closing the blade in the backswing and consequently swinging from closed to open.

Work on opening the blade going back, so that in position 2 the toe points upward and slightly behind you. On the forward swing, think of rolling the right forearm over the left, or working the toe of the club past the heel—either of these thoughts will induce the correct rotation to the left. Find out which one best works for you.

If the whole action still seems a little stiff, then study your arm action. On the backswing, the right arm should fold while the left arm stays extended. On the downswing, the right arm should extend as the left arm folds. Many seniors make the mistake of not folding the right arm enough going back or not folding the left arm enough in the follow-through. The stiffness this puts in the swing prevents a free release of the arms. You'll find that, if you allow the right arm to fold a little more on the backswing, and the left arm to fold a little more going through, you can now release the club fast and freely.

Even exaggerate these actions for a while until you start to get results. Grip so lightly that the club could be knocked out of your hands. Then you'll get plenty of wrist and "folding" action. Also, overdo the arm rotation to the right going back and to the left going through. Don't worry: The worst thing that can happen is that you'll hook the ball. Once you know what too much rotation to the left is, you can easily learn to rotate a little less. Then you'll get a draw instead of a hook! As you know, that's exactly what I want you to learn to do.

Once you've experienced the feel of good hand action, then you should work on the "Walk-Through" action. Hopefully, by this point, you'll have "walked through" a couple of shots quite naturally. However, if you haven't, don't despair. Remember: You may have spent years doing that "reverse-C" swing, and keeping the upper body behind the ball has become pretty well ingrained. If so, I have just the thing for you.

**The "Walk-Through" Drill.** Take a short iron, and hit some balls from a slight downhill lie, as I am doing in the photos, even if the downhill aspect isn't particularly evident. You'll find that, as long as you key on going down the slope after the ball, you'll quite naturally walk through the ball in the follow-

*To learn the "Walk-Through," practice from a slightly downhill lie.*

through. Your right foot will step directly over the left foot on a line parallel to your intended line of swing and you'll finish in the correct, erect position. You may stop right there or keep on walking—either is fine. Like the other drills, the "Walk-Through" drill will force you to make the right action so you can build up the correct feel.

It's worth noting that swing computers show that the best golfers make a big weight shift both ways. They have 90 percent of the weight on the right foot at the top, and 90 percent on the left foot at impact. This "back and through" shifting of weight is what gives you the leverage needed in the downswing. The "Walk-Through" action ensures you have practically all your weight on the left foot at impact and so gives you the ultimate in leverage.

## Pull All the Way Through

FOR the strongest type of hit, you not only need the counterclockwise rotation of the left arm and hand through impact, you should also continue to pull through with the left hand all

*To develop a wide follow-through, practice the "let go" drill.*

the way into the finish. This gives you as wide a follow-through as possible, and when you have that, you'll be keeping the club moving through impact as fast as you personally can. That compresses the ball to the maximum. Although, as a senior, your follow-through may not be quite as wide as it used to be, nevertheless you should work on making it as wide as possible.

To convey this idea to the senior with whom I'm working, I tell him to imagine his left hand is a car that he must "park" in a "garage" on the "top floor," above his left shoulder. He should never "park" it low, in the "basement," which would be a short, narrow, choppy follow-through. However, I've found that many still need a little help in getting the right idea. So here it is.

**The "Let-Go" Drill.** Take a regular backswing, but then let go of the club with your right hand at impact. As you swing through, you'll feel the correct "pull through" action of the left hand. Although I had to pose the accompanying photos in order to get exactly the right pictures, I think you can get the idea of it. Make dry runs at first, in other words, swing without a ball. Initially, do the drill with a driver. You'll find that the extra length of the club really conveys the "pull through" feel.

The "pull through" action is equally important with irons, and of course, it's far easier at first to hit balls "letting go" with a short iron. If most of your weight is on your left foot at impact, as it should be, and you're pulling through, then you'll take long, shallow divots. I recently measured my divots made hitting a 5-iron and found that they were about six inches long and an eighth of an inch deep. This type of divot proves that you're pulling through the ball all the way into the finish. Short, deep divots indicate too steep a descent and a narrow follow-through with no "pull through."

One of the reasons many of you seniors make a restricted follow-through is that you've never learned to trust the loft on the club to get the ball up. You try to "scoop" the ball up with the right hand, narrowing the follow-through, instead of pulling through with the left. You'll get a lot of thin shots this way, and will sometimes even top the ball. If this is your problem, then this drill is for you.

**Hit under the String.** Set two stakes in the ground about six feet apart and tie string to them so that the string is about a foot above the ground. Then take an iron and set up with the length of string to your left across and at right angles to your intended

*A super senior (sixty-five years and up) should take a narrower stance, and "drag" the clubhead away. You then get a super "pull down" and a strong "whip lash" action with the hands and arms through the ball.*

line of swing. Place the string/stake arrangement sufficiently far ahead of your ball so that you won't snag it with the club in the follow-through. Then, hit some balls, trying to drive each ball *under* the middle of the string. You won't be able to do it, of course, but the effort to do so will make you pull through strongly with the left hand, cutting that long, thin divot.

**Hit Irons from a Bunker.** While I'm talking about irons, let me tell you of another little trick I've found useful myself and which has really helped many of my senior friends. If you want to improve your iron play, then try hitting some clean iron shots from a bunker. Take, say, ten balls into a bunker and hit them out with a 7-iron. This drill trains you to shift the weight to the left foot, so that you catch the ball first, and then take the divot. The moment you hit behind the ball, or "fat" as it is often called, you know immediately, because the ball goes nowhere!

The first time you try it, you're likely to hit seven balls "fat." But don't give up. My personal best is nine good ones out of ten! I've never quite mastered this one, but it's fun and very educational to try!

I made use of this idea just before I won the 1959 British

Open. I hadn't been hitting my irons cleanly and so I went down to the beach near Muirfield and hit a lot of irons. With a few hours practice on the sand, my iron play was ready!

## SUPER SENIORS

ALTHOUGH you can continue to use the "Walk-Through" swing for the rest of your golfing life, here are a few modifications that will help the super senior, say, a person of sixty years of age, and up.

Your swing, with age, will become a bit shorter, especially if you don't exercise. If your swing shortens, then you'll have to either accept it or do some exercise. (See the second half of this book.) Whatever you do, don't try to fake a longer back-swing by "lifting" with the arms, for example, or bending the left arm excessively. As I told you earlier, these faults give you a narrow backswing, no windup, and you'll come down "wide," with no power. A correct, but shorter, swing will always be more powerful and reliable than a longer, faked swing.

With age, the swing also becomes more and more an arms and hands effort, because you eventually can't use the lower body as effectively as you once could. When you reach this point, narrow the stance still more and use a slight lag of the clubhead in the takeaway, as I'm demonstrating in the photos. If you drag the clubhead away last from the ball, you'll get a super "pull down" from the top. You'll increase your wrist cock on the downswing and get a "whip lash" action through the ball that will give you maximum power.

On the PGA Tour, long-hitting Danny Pohl uses this action. Study his swing if you get the chance.

## One Thought at a Time

ALTHOUGH I've necessarily gone into a lot of detail in this chapter, I hope you haven't gotten the impression that you should think of all this out on the course. You should work on your swing away from the course—at home and on the practice ground. If you want to improve, you're going to have to make time for this.

Before you hit the ball during a round, it's fine to think of a swing key as you make a practice swing. In fact, I'd encourage you to do so. Practice swings are important for seniors because they keep you loose, and you might as well kill two birds with one stone.

However, when you're ready to make your shot, just concentrate on mental pictures of your ball going to the target. If you try to cram the brain with twenty swing keys, you'll thoroughly confuse yourself, and your body won't perform as it should. Even if you only try to think of one swing key during an actual shot, most of the time you may perform the key well, but the rest of the swing will fall apart.

As the old saying goes, "You've got to dance with the girl you've brung!" Translated to golf, this means that when hitting shots on the course, you *must* trust your swing. You've built up muscle memory with the drills. Now you have to *let* your swing happen, not *make* it happen.

CHAPTER FIVE

# GET THE RIGHT EQUIPMENT

$\int$OME YEARS AGO, in 1964, I was playing in the Pensacola Open. In the middle of the first round, the weather suddenly turned colder. I was caught playing with my regular driver, which had a very stiff shaft. Also, the only balls I had in my bag were 100 compression. Now, cold weather not only makes a hard ball like a "100" feel like a rock, it also stiffens the steel in the club shaft. So, all my drives from then on felt like I was hitting one rock with another! It wasn't very comfortable and I didn't, as I remember, score too well. The next day, I was better prepared. I took 90 compression balls out with me along with my "cold day" driver, one with a slightly "softer," that is, more flexible, shaft. I played very, very well that day, and the next. The final day, it warmed up again and I could return to my regular driver and the harder balls. I tied Arnold Palmer and Miller Barber at 274, and won the playoff.

I doubt if I could have won had I not had the second driver available. The moral of the story is that, while you can't buy a golf swing with a new set of clubs, having the right equipment on hand for your game can be worth several shots a round.

I often see seniors continuing to play with the same type of equipment as when younger. In many cases, this equipment no longer suits them and/or there have been equipment advances that would really help them, if they would but take advantage

> **Seniors: If you have 1-, 2-, and 3-irons of any sort, get rid of them! Replace them with 5- and 7-woods or a utility wood.**

of them. Another side of the story is to have properly fitted clubs with specs that give you the right shape of shot, which, as I've explained, should be a draw. Let's explore these topics now in more detail.

## THE RIGHT STUFF

YOU may have been able to play long irons well when younger, but as you get on in years, you'll find it more and more difficult to generate strong enough hand action to get the ball up high enough. So, the first order of business for a senior is to replace the 1-, 2-, and 3-irons with woods like the 5- and 7-wood or one of the newer utility woods, most of which have a 4-wood length with a 7-wood loft. You'll find that it is infinitely easier to get the ball up with these well lofted woods, and from the rough they perform so much better than a long iron. By the way, I'd include in this prohibition of long irons even the cavity-back or hollow irons that have appeared in recent years.

I definitely think that seniors should play with metal woods and a two-piece, Surlyn-covered ball. First, metal woods are proven on the tours. I think this is most important. If so many top players are using them, including Lee Trevino and Curtis Strange on the PGA Tour, Bruce Crampton, Don January, and Dale Douglas on the Senior PGA Tour, and Juli Inkster, Betsy King, and Jane Geddes on the LPGA Tour, then the senior simply can't ignore them. Second, metal woods are perimeter weighted. This means they're more forgiving on off-center hits than most "wood" woods. (It's worth noting that graphite-headed and ceramic woods are also perimeter weighted.) Third, the combination of a metal wood and a Surlyn two-piece ball gives you the most distance. It's true that you can't put as much backspin on a Surlyn two-piece ball as on a balata-covered wound ball or even a Surlyn-covered wound ball, but for a senior the highest priority is maximum distance.

A few years ago, I was playing in a pro-am and one of my partners was a man in his sixties. He asked me, "How do you put so much stop on the ball with your 3-iron?" I replied, "I hit the ball very late. I catch the ball first. I hit down and through, and it stops." He then asked me, "How far do you hit the 3-iron?" I said, "190–200 yards. How far do you hit yours?" He said, "150 yards." I then had to ask him, "Well, why do you want the ball to stop?!"

Another way of putting it is that most seniors come up short of the pin on their approaches, anyway. So, most of the time using a Surlyn ball that will release a little after hitting the green rather than stopping or sucking back is, on average, going to do them the most good.

Another plus of either Surlyn ball is that you get less side-spin with it than a balata ball. This means that you minimize unwanted slices and hooks. It's true that for the same reason, you can't work the ball—deliberately hook or slice it—as much, either. However, for most seniors this is less important.

Although I don't think it's mandatory to go to the so-called "game-improvement" irons, they certainly are worth considering. While the classic blade does give you more distance and better feedback, cavity back and hollow irons are, like metal woods, perimeter weighted and thus more forgiving on mishits. So, if you only play a very little, or you're not a very accurate striker of the ball, they're well worth a try.

Whichever type of iron you use, I've found it a good idea to find the "sweet spot" on the blade and mark it with, say, paint on the top edge. (The sweet spot is the clubhead's center of gravity in the toe-to-heel direction.) Then you can line up the sweet spot with the center of the ball at address. To find the sweet spot, hold the club at the butt end with your index finger and thumb, and let the club hang. Then tap along the face with a pencil until you find the spot where your tapping neither opens or closes the club. That's the sweet spot. It's worth adding that, if your putter doesn't have a mark on top showing the sweet spot, or if you suspect the mark is in the wrong place— very common with older putters—you should adopt the same procedure as with the irons.

In recent years, several new shaft materials, all very expensive, have come along to challenge steel. Today, we have boron shafts, graphite shafts, titanium shafts, and others. Because they're lighter than steel, these shafts are often touted as giving increased distance. So, shouldn't a senior golfer adopt them?

As regards the boron and graphite shafts, the problem is that they have more torque than steel. In other words, the force of the swing makes them twist the clubface open going back, and closed going through. Unless you are a very smooth swinger in the Bob Jones mold, you have a serious control problem. The ones I've tried recently still have too much torque and person-

---

**Seniors: If you have trouble getting the ball up in the air, then try metal woods, and sole-weighted or perimeter-weighted irons.**

ally I'm going to wait on boron and graphite until the manufacturers produce a shaft with torque resistance equal to steel.

I feel that if these shafts were that good, then all the top tour players would be using them. However, up to now, the majority of leading players in the world all continue to use steel shafts despite the growing popularity of new shaft materials. As a rule of thumb, it would be wise for you to play with the same type of shaft that the top players do, and that's steel. I would especially recommend Northwestern's Power Kick shaft to average seniors.

Having said this, I will admit that you see a lot of graphite and boron shafts out on the LPGA Tour. The reason for this is not difficult to deduce. The women simply don't swing as powerfully as men and thus the shafts don't twist as much because the swing forces acting on them aren't as strong.

What's sauce for the goose is sauce for the gander, right? So, by my own rule of thumb, you women should definitely look into graphite shafts. However, if the shaft suits you, get a complete set of graphite-shafted clubs. Don't just get a graphite-shafted driver, because it won't match your other clubs. With today's advanced "frequency matching" of shafts, you'd do far better with a matched set of lightweight steel-shafted clubs.

The same thinking would apply to male seniors, who are not long hitters.

I don't have the same reservation about titanium shafts because their torque resistance is better than steel shafts. Several PGA Tour players played with the shaft when they were available a few years ago. Now, during the last year they're again being manufactured. However, I'd only recommend them if, again, you can afford a complete set. And if you are in the market for a new set, Pat McPherson, my dear friend in Dundee, Scotland, contends that dark or matt clubs are preferable, as clubs with a high finish can create a glare in the sun.

One question that I often get asked is what to look for in a sand wedge. A good sand wedge must have what is known as "bounce." In other words, the sole should angle down from the leading edge to the rear of the sole so that when you set the club down squarely at address, the back of the sole is on the ground, but the leading edge is raised off the ground. "Bounce" is what enables the sand wedge to skid through the sand, rather than cutting down into it. As a general rule, go for a sand wedge with a medium width of sole—don't go to extremes such as very wide or very narrow soles. Having said this, I should add that, if your bunkers have coarser, harder sand or there's not much depth of sand, then a narrower-soled sand wedge will do better for you. Seniors, I find, are invariably short playing out of greenside bunkers—possibly this is because they've lost a little strength and simply misjudge how hard they need to hit the ball. At any rate it's a good idea for seniors to use a sand wedge with less loft than usual—say, 54–55 degrees rather than 56–57.

The "bounce" that makes a good sand wedge will also make it more difficult to play from grass. As a general rule, you should only use a sand wedge that has "bounce" from a good lie, or from rough where you can slip the club under the ball. This is especially true if you're opening the blade, which raises the leading edge still higher. Attempting to play a sand wedge from a bare lie is very difficult unless you play it back in the stance, with your hands ahead hooding the blade. However, then you've taken so much loft off the club, there's not much point in playing it.

I think the short game is so important for seniors that a good case can be made for carrying a third wedge. This club should have about the same amount of loft as your sand wedge, but have a fairly narrow, flat sole, that is, it should have no "bounce." You'll then have no trouble with short pitches from practically any lie.

When it comes to putters, I think that seniors should take advantage of the heel-toe weighted putters which have become so popular in recent years. The heel-toe weighting means that you get almost the same result whether you hit the ball exactly right, on the sweet spot of the putter, or mishit it on the toe or heel. *You can't afford to give any type of advantage to an opponent!* The best putters on the PGA Tour, including Tom Watson, use heel-toe weighted putters. So should you.

Having said this, I must admit that I don't follow my own advice on this particular point! I'm still using an old blade putter I acquired in 1961. I can't tell you what make it is, because there's no name on it. It has a plain blade—no heel-toe weighting. If you asked me why, I'd have to admit that it was a love affair. I simply fell in love with that old putter years ago and, when you do that, it's the exception that proves the rule. People have compared finding a good putter to finding a good wife or husband, and I don't think they're far from wrong!

Actually, I've found three other putters that look very similar to my "old Faithful." I'm now in the process of building up a second set of clubs in case something happens to mine. I've never done that before, but really it's stupid of me not to have done so.

For example, after winning the 1987 U.S. Senior Open in

Fairfield, CT, there was great confusion as Vivienne and I rushed off to go to the British Senior Open, played the following week. I thought that someone had put my clubs in the courtesy car. Then, as I was halfway to the airport, I thought, "We'd better stop and double-check that the clubs are in the trunk." They weren't! After a frantic phone call to the Brooklawn CC, the police took charge of my clubs and gave them an escort right to the plane! If it hadn't been for the police, I might well have landed in Britain without my clubs!

I'm deeply grateful to the police for the marvellous work they normally do at golf tournaments. However, this effort was really above and beyond the call of duty, and I'd like to take this opportunity to thank them for it.

## THE RIGHT FIT

WHEN selecting new clubs, you should be aware that you can ask your club professional for various club specifications—namely lie, face angle on woods, grip size and positioning and shaft flex—that make it easier to draw the ball, the shape of shot that's best for seniors. He can also change the specs of your current clubs.

For example, most seniors slice the ball. If you slice, help yourself to draw the ball by having your clubs bent to a more upright lie by your pro. About 1 degree more upright is about right. If you're fairly short like myself, and have been using clubs that are 2 degrees flatter than standard, try clubs only 1 degree flat. If you're tall, and have been using a standard lie in the past, try 1 degree upright.

If you slice, you should also ask your pro to check whether your present woods have square, open, or closed clubfaces. If your current clubs have square or open faces, then you should change them for clubs with more closed faces.

The way the grip is set on the club can also help you draw the ball. Many seniors like the type of grip that has a straight rib along the bottom of the grip. Normally, the rib is centered on the underside of the grip. However, if you set the rib slightly off center, that is, to the hole side of center as you grip the club, this helps you take a strong grip on the club, and therefore draw the ball. This adjustment is known as "setting the grip strong."

The size of the grip is also important. The thicker the grip, the more it reduces the rotation of the left arm to the left through the ball (also known as "hand action"), the motion that closes the clubface through impact. Smaller grips, on the other hand, increase this rotation. You get more hand action and a faster release. So, if you need some help in drawing the ball, try slightly thinner grips.

The most important specification to get right is shaft flex. Here I don't agree that senior golfers should follow the common advice of going to very flexible shafts. I've always used very stiff shafts, and thanks to my exercises with a heavy club and others, I still find them best for me. I feel that the more flexible the shaft, the harder it is to control and the more smoothly and perfectly you have to swing. With very flexible shafts, there's too little margin for error for the average senior.

Basically, I feel that if you need help from your equipment in drawing the ball, you'll do better to change the lie, the clubface and your grip first, as I've described above. This is especially true if you're getting good control with your current shafts.

However, let me paint another scenario for you. If you used, say, stiff shafts when younger, and now you're leaving every ball to the right, then it may be time to go to a *slightly* more flexible shaft, say, a regular shaft. Slightly more shaft flex will kick the clubhead into the ball a little quicker through impact, closing the face a little and helping you draw the ball.

Funnily enough, I have recently gone to a heavier set of irons, not lighter, as you might expect. Purely by chance, Northwestern happened to send me a set of irons that were D-4 in swingweight, and I just love them. Yet, up to that time, I'd always used much lighter clubs, with a D-0 swingweight. I can't account for why I like them. Whether they make me swing a little slower—essential when you're under pressure— I don't know, but they feel just great.

If you've lost length over the years, a lot of people will tell you to try clubs with longer shafts. Here I should warn against merely sticking a wood extension in the butt end of the grip as a permanent solution. When you increase the length of the shaft in this way, you increase the swingweight of the club—it will feel heavier—and you also increase the flexibility of the shaft. You're quite likely to experience a loss of control. It's fine to do this with an old club just to see if this will give you a little more distance. If you still want to go ahead with longer clubs, then get shafts (or new clubs with such shafts) that will have the right flex for you at the longer length as well as the right swingweight.

You should also not go to extremes. It's true that a longer club will give you more leverage, and therefore you have the potential to hit the ball farther. However, there's a definite tradeoff in accuracy. The longer the club, the harder it is to hit the ball on the sweet spot of the club. With clubs two inches longer than standard, for example, you might easily miss two drives out of three. This is too big a price to pay for that one drive that goes a few yards farther. That's why you should try clubs no more than a half an inch to an inch longer than your current set. Even then, the person who has the best chance of making longer clubs work is one with a smooth, Gene Littler-type swing.

Finally, a couple of thoughts on two unsung heroes in equipment—your shoes and your glove.

Always get shoes with as wide a sole and heel as you can find. This gives you the firmest possible stance and helps you maintain your balance.

I consider a glove very important to holding onto the club better. I'm not alone in this belief—just about every tour golfer uses one. You get far better adhesion between a grip and a glove than between a grip and the bare hand.

However, some seniors, I know, prefer not to use a glove, perhaps because they couldn't afford it when younger or because their hero when growing up was Ben Hogan, who never wore a glove. Today, on the Senior Tour, we have another marvellous player, namely Bruce Crampton, who also doesn't use a glove. Whatever the reason for your not wearing a glove, I do suggest that you at least get a special "rainy day" glove, available from your pro, and keep it in your bag at all times. This type of glove enables you to hang onto the club even when both the grip and glove are soaked.

You'll bless me the next time you're caught in the rain!

## KEEP AN OPEN MIND

PERHAPS the most important thing I can tell you about equipment is to experiment and keep an open mind. I've given you my views here, but you must feel free to disagree, because good equipment, like beauty, is so often in the eye of the beholder. My old putter is a good example of this!

One thing is certain: New equipment is coming along all the time, and it's constantly improving. Believe me, you owe it to yourself to try new clubs, new balls, and use them if they improve your game. Don't hesitate to pick your pro's brains on this—that's one of the reasons he's there, to help you play better.

When I remember the golf balls that I played with as a young man, there's no doubt in my mind that the modern balls not only fly farther, they're far more consistent. Clubs have also improved out of all recognition.

I often hear people saying that today's players on the PGA Tour are so much better than the heroes of yesteryear. That's boloney! The low scoring today is the result of new and better equipment and the fine manicuring of tour courses. Period!

There is a tremendous *depth* of talent today on the PGA Tour. That's true. However, if Ben Hogan, Sam Snead, and Byron Nelson were now in their prime, and you gave them new clubs, and let them play with modern balls, which go as much as 20 yards farther, on today's finely conditioned golf courses, the top young players of today would have a hard time keeping up with them!

I know. I've played golf with all three of them.

## CHAPTER SIX

# WORK THE BALL

I SAID EARLIER THAT, for many seniors, working the ball to the left or right, or hitting it high or low is probably less important than raw distance. I'll stand by that remark. However, here I would like to try to persuade you to at least try these shots in practice.

We professionals need to learn to work the ball, not just for the obvious reason—to hit a ball around or over or under a tree—but to deal with many other shot-making situations. For example, we play to a lot of greens where the officials "tuck" the pins behind bunkers or close to water. To get the ball close —safely—we then have to draw or fade the ball so that it lands on the middle of the green and then kicks to the left or right to the pin. We also fade or draw the ball into cross winds to hold the ball straight and drop it onto the green under perfect control. We develop high, soft shots to deal with hard greens, and low shots to deal with wind.

For most seniors, just developing a reasonably straight ball is difficult enough. They seldom get to the stage where, like professionals, they have the skill to work the ball. However, the reason why I'm asking you to practice deliberate hooks, slices, high, and low shots is *not* so that you can pull off one or two extraordinarily fine shots on the course. That will be the icing on the cake. Rather, it's because, by working on these shots, you're going to understand your swing better and ultimately improve it.

Many seniors are either unaware of the type of swing they have—and the usual ball flight it produces—or have lived with it so long they no longer notice it. I want you to *know* what you're doing. Then, you can work out where you should go from there.

I think it's interesting that this type of "blindness" doesn't only afflict the casual amateur. We professionals suffer from it, too. Remember what I told you earlier about the incident at the 1978 Masters, when I never realized I had let my ball position creep forward so much that I couldn't hook the ball? That's one example. Another affected is no less a golfer than Arnold Palmer.

Arnold is one of the great drawers of the ball. He has done it all his life. If, for my life, I had to select one man to hook a ball around a tree and onto a green, I'd take Arnold every time. Well, back in the early sixties, he and I were partners in the Challenge Golf series, in which we challenged other teams. Every now and again, he'd say to me something like, "Gary, I think this 3-wood shot requires a fade." I'd say, "Yes, it does." He'd then take his 3-wood and knock the ball right on the green, *but the ball still flew a bit from right to left!* He'd then say to me, "Did you like that fade, Gary?" Out loud I'd say, "That was a very pretty shot," but to myself I'd say, "I love it, it's on the green, but it didn't fade!" Of course, one must never say anything that would upset one's partner. However, I think it's interesting that, to Arnold's eyes, the ball obviously did appear to fade left to right whereas I knew very well it clearly had flown the opposite way!

If you find it difficult to hook the ball, for example, it's because your regular swing produces a fade, as mine did that time at Augusta, or even a slice. If you slice, you'll find that, initially, you have to exaggerate the factors that will produce the hook. Most seniors in fact do slice, and, as you've seen, I want you to learn the draw, so, covering this problem thoroughly will be very important to the majority of you. Similarly, a few of you may find it difficult to fade or slice the ball at first. If so, then, like Arnold Palmer, your normal swing is probably of the draw/hook type.

The same type of thinking applies to low and high shots. If you normally hit the ball too low, you'll find this out very rapidly if you follow the instructions to hit the ball low—

---

**Seniors: Most of you have got so used to your normal swing, you no longer "see" the hook or slice it produces or whether you hit the ball too high or low. There's one way to tell for certain—ask your professional to check it. Then, you can work on improving your swing.**

you'll hit a "wormburner!" If you normally hit the ball too high, and follow the instructions on hitting it high, you could easily top it!

## DRAWS AND HOOKS

IF you presently hit the ball fairly straight, then to draw or hook the ball, all you do is to take a stronger grip, aim the club slightly right of target, and set up with your feet and shoulders aligned parallel to that intended line of swing, to the right of target. In other words, you set up as though you were going to play the shot straight to the right of target. However, because of the stronger grip, you increase the rotation of the left arm—to the right going back and to the left going through. This rotation closes the clubface at impact and you draw or hook the ball. Because you swing through to the right of the target, that's where the ball starts. Because the club is closed at impact, hookspin takes over later in the flight of the ball and brings the ball back from the right to the target.

You control the amount of curve from right to left with your grip. For a draw, use a slightly stronger grip, as described earlier. If you want a hook, simply take an even stronger grip, increasing the rotation and closing the clubface still more at

To hook the ball, aim right, take a lighter, stronger grip. Play the ball back in the stance. Swing back to the inside, rotating the left arm to the right more than usual. At the top, feel as though you're "crossing the line." Then swing in to out, rotating the left arm to the left more than usual.

impact. Of course, on a hook, you have to aim farther to the right to allow for the bigger curve.

In the photos, I am hitting a hook. Note how far I'm aiming to the right of the target to allow for the big curve ball I'm going to get. I've set up with the feet and shoulders parallel to my intended line of swing to the right. It looks as though I'm going to hit the shot straight to the right into the trees that line the right side of the fairway, and that's how I feel. I don't change anything in the address other than taking a much stronger grip. The swing follows the setup. I feel as though I'm swinging normally—it's just that I'm swinging back and through to the right of target. However, because of the stronger grip, I'll rotate the club slightly more to the right going back and slightly more to the left going through.

If you look at the last two photos in the series, you can see what I mean. In this position where the club is horizontal to the ground, the "straight ball" position would find the toe pointing straight up. For a draw, as I've previously stated, you rotate the club more to the left, so that the toe points slightly behind the player and the face of the club faces very slightly down. Now, for a hook, you've increased the rotation to the left still more, so that the clubface faces more downward than for the draw.

If these instructions don't give you the desired draw or hook, then your normal swing is of the fade or slice type. Adjusting

your aim and strengthening the grip by themselves are not enough to make you draw or hook the ball. In fact, you may simply push it to the right. This is because you've grooved a swing where you play the ball too far forward, take the club back outside the line, and then never release—there's no rotation of the left arm to the left on the downswing.

To get the ball to curve to the left, you'll have to work on some additional points: Play the ball farther back in your stance, take the club definitely to the inside, make certain you roll the clubface open going back, feel as though you're "crossing the line" at the top, and make a big effort to roll the left arm to the left through the ball. You'll find it helpful to work on the "feet together" drill I mentioned earlier; this helps you develop the necessary arm rotation and hand action. You may also find that using a far lighter grip than normal frees up your arms so that they can rotate freely. Most slicers grip far too tightly.

It's worth repeating that, when drawing or hooking the ball, you shouldn't approach the ball from directly behind it, on a line directly from the ball to the target. Rather, you should approach it from a spot slightly left of that line. Then, you see clearly how far right of target you want to aim, and be able to set up square to that aiming point.

## FADES AND SLICES

IF you normally hit a fairly straight ball, then if you want to fade or slice take a weaker grip, aim the club left of target, then set up with your feet and shoulders aligned parallel to that intended line of swing, to the left of target. It's as though you were going to play a straight shot left of target, but the weaker grip will cause a reverse rotation of the left arm, that is, to the right (clockwise) going through the ball, opening the blade. The ball starts to the left, because that's the direction in which you're swinging. However, because the clubface is open at impact, you put slice spin on the ball, and it then curves back to the right.

As with the hook, you control the amount of curve with your grip. For a fade, use a grip that is only a little weaker. For a slice, take a still weaker grip, increasing the reverse rotation of the left arm through the ball.

In the photos, I am hitting a slice. I've set up well to the left of the ultimate target. The swing feels normal except that the

*To slice the ball, aim left, take a tighter, weaker grip. Play the ball more forward. Swing back to the outside. At the top, feel as though you're in a "laid off" position. On the downswing, swing out to in. Keep the clubface open through impact by pulling the club across the ball.*

direction of the swing follows the setup—I've swung back and through to the left of target.

If these instructions don't make you fade or slice the ball, then this is because you normally draw or hook the ball; aiming left and weakening the grip will not be enough to get you the desired fade or slice. In fact, you may simply pull the ball to the left. This is because in your normal swing you play the ball too far back, take the club way inside and "cross the line" at the top. You come into the ball very much from in to out and have a big rotation of the left arm to the left through impact.

To get the slice spin you're looking for, you may also have to do the following: Play the ball farther forward in the stance, work on taking the club back outside to what feels like a "lay off" position, and make certain you keep the clubface open through impact. You'll probably have to tighten up your grip, especially that of the left hand, and work on pulling the club across the ball with almost a sawing motion. You can see this "pull across" action in the last two photos in the series. Especially study the face of the club, it's in the "slice" position, "looking" upward to the sky.

As you did with the draw, adjust the position from which you start your pre-shot routine behind the ball. Approach the ball from a position slightly right of the direct line from ball to target so that you can easily aim left of target and set up parallel to that aim.

## HIGH AND LOW SHOTS

HITTING the ball high and low is primarily a matter of adjusting your ball position and weight.

To hit the ball higher than usual, move the ball a little forward in your stance, farther up toward the left foot, and drop your right shoulder slightly lower at address. This has the ef-

*To hit the high shot, play the ball forward, keep the weight on the right foot.*

*To hit the low shot, play the ball back, keep the weight cn the left foot.*

fect of placing more of your weight behind the ball, on the right foot. Instead of the shaft leaning slightly forward at address and impact as on a normal shot, it's just about vertical when you view the golfer from in front, as I'm demonstrating in the photo. This increases the effective loft of the club. During the swing, you work on keeping your weight back so that you strike the ball with the increased loft and a sweeping blow.

To hit a low shot, do just the opposite. Play the ball back in your stance, move it toward the right foot, and level your shoulders. This puts more of your weight ahead of the ball on your left foot. For the low shot, the shaft leans forward, and your hands are well ahead of the ball. This reduces the effective loft of the club. During the swing, you work on keeping the weight on the left foot so you hit the ball with the reduced loft and a descending blow.

If you normally hit the ball on a good trajectory, neither too high nor low, then these instructions will give you the desired higher or lower shot. However, if you normally hit the ball too low or high, and don't know it, you'll soon see your error when you attempt these shots.

For example, if your normal shot is too high, then you already play the ball forward and have too much weight behind the ball. When you attempt to play it farther forward, putting more weight on the right foot, you hit the ball on the upswing so much that you hit the ball thin or even top it. If this happens, then you know your normal shot is too high. Try a low shot for confirmation, playing the ball back and putting more weight on the left foot. If you then hit a much stronger shot than usual, the ball flying lower but farther than usual, you know that your normal shot was too high.

The same thing will happen in reverse if, unwittingly, you hit your normal shot too low. You'll attempt the low shot, and play the ball so far back, you'll barely get it airborne. Attempt the high shot, and you'll get a far better, stronger trajectory and more carry.

## GET HOOKED

ONCE you start practicing deliberate hooks and slices, and low and high shots, I think you'll get "hooked" on it. A golfer who can work the ball has so many more options in a particular situation than a player who can only play one type of shot. The game becomes a lot more fun. You'll not only develop a better swing, you'll become a "player."

It's never too late to learn.

## CHAPTER SEVEN

# PLAY THE PERCENTAGES

RECENTLY, I was playing in a pro-am and one of my partners, a man in his fifties, asked me, "Gary, what's the biggest difference between the way professionals play and us amateurs?" I think he was expecting to hear something like, "Professionals hit it farther, miss fewer shots, or have better touch around the greens." However, the more I thought about his question, the more I realized that none of these was really the right answer. The biggest difference is this: A professional plays percentage golf; most senior amateurs don't.

Everything the professional does is designed to give him the best chance of playing well. He warms up before his round, he plans his strategy for every hole, he's acutely aware of his present level of skill, he plays to make the most of his assets and avoid his weaknesses, he invariably plays the best percentage shot, he leaves nothing to chance. In short, he's organized.

I'm convinced that playing the percentages by itself could drop the handicaps of many of you seniors by several strokes. So, let's discuss it.

## WARM UP

"I played badly for the first five holes, but from then on, I played pretty well." If you find yourself saying this at the nineteenth hole, then I know what your problem is—you simply didn't warm up before your round.

No professional would make this mistake. From the golfing point of view, your muscles won't perform well if they're cold. Also, if you make too much demand on your muscles when cold, you can hurt yourself. I think one of the reasons why there are so few injuries on tour is simply that every professional warms up before his round.

If a tour player finds it essential to warm up, it surely goes double for any senior. The joints and muscles tend to get stiffer with age. So, avoid arriving at the course at the last moment before your tee time. Give yourself the time for a warmup, and you'll play up to your potential right from the first tee.

You may have noticed that the way we professionals warm up is first to go to the practice ground and work up through our bag. We'll hit a few little wedge shots, then work up to a full wedge, then hit a few shots with each club until we come to the driver. Then, we may hit a few more little wedges and bunker shots before going to the practice green. There we'll practice some chip shots as well as putts. I'd suggest that you, too, make the time for a good warmup and use exactly the same procedure. However, if you're a little short of time, simply hit representative clubs, such as the wedge, 8-iron, 5-iron, fairway wood, and driver, rather than every club in the bag.

Here let me give you a little tip. Whatever you do, don't hit too many drives—half a dozen is quite enough—and never hit more than one drive at a time! If you hit drive after drive, you'll tend to speed up your tempo. All of us, when we get that club in our hands, find it difficult to resist the tendency to crush it! This defeats one of the major purposes of the warmup, which is to get comfortable with your swing on that day and reestablish good tempo. Instead, hit a few shots with a fairway wood, then hit a drive with exactly the same swing. Keep on alternating drives with your fairway woods, and you'll retain your tempo.

I should add that on cold days, you're going to take longer to warm up your muscles. So, plan on some extra time. On very hot days, the reverse is true. Take far fewer full swings. You're going to loosen up very quickly, and, if you hit flat out for too long, you may well leave your best shots on the practice ground.

Another tip is always, but always, to give yourself enough time to play some short shots. If you analyse your mistakes early in the round, I'll bet that you miss a lot of greens. If your short game is sharp and ready to go, you can get the ball up and down. If it's "cold," you're in trouble!

A very good way to warm up your short game, and one that is economical on time, is to use three or four balls, but hit each one to a different hole on the practice green. This puts you immediately into a "game" frame of mind. Out on the course, you only get one chance to play the shot, so you might as well prepare for it. As the old Scottish pros used to say, "Any bloody fool can do it the second time!"

First, hit some wedge shots, then go to the edge of the practice green, and hit some chips, followed by some long putts. In each case, make one shot as different as possible from the next —one might be uphill, the next sidehill, the next downhill, one longer, one shorter, and so on. Finish with those "miss-able" putts, in the six- to ten-foot range—the type of putt you'll soon face if you don't make a good pitch or chip. Here, you can play to the same hole as long as you play each ball from a different side of the cup.

Sometimes, I know, you're going to turn up at the club with only a few minutes to spare! If you get caught in that fix, then here are a few exercises that will at least limber up the muscles. First, put a club behind your back and support it with the crook of your arms as I'm doing in the photos. From an

*Warm up drill: With a club behind your back, turn right and left. Repeat.*

*Warm up drill: Swing two clubs back and through until you're loose.*

address position, turn to the right and then to the left. Second, take two or three clubs (or slip one of those donut-shaped warm-up weights on your driver) and swing them back and through. Initially, do these exercises very slowly and don't fully extend the muscles until you feel you can comfortably do so. I repeat, as you get older, you must be careful not to ask too much of your muscles when they're cold or only partially warmed up. When you're fully loosened up, then take a couple of real practice swings with a driver, using full power. A good tip here is to swing at a tee peg stuck in the ground. Then, you'll pay far more attention to getting your address correct and the swing itself will be far more realistic.

## PLAN YOUR ROUND

BEN HOGAN did it, I do it, I think just about every professional does it—we plan our round. If you want to get the most out of your game, then you seniors should do it, too.

When you have a moment, sit down in an easy chair, relax, and mentally go out to the first tee of your golf course. Play each hole in your mind, assessing the trouble, the best position for the tee shot, the fat portion of the green, the side of the green, if any, on which it's best to miss the approach shot, even, say, any 3-putt positions on the green.

Let's say the first hole is a par 4. The ground is flat from the tee up to the landing area, which is flanked by two bunkers on either side of the fairway. Trees line the rough on both sides from a point just beyond the fairway bunkers to a point just short of the green. From the flat portion, the fairway goes down into a valley and then up to the green. This is protected by a big bunker on the left side and another, smaller one guarding the right front.

Cast your mind back to the times when you played the hole best, and worst. You might come up with something like the following:

"I got a birdie one time when I hit a great drive. It hit the flat portion of the fairway and rolled down the hill. I then hit a great 9-iron from a downhill lie six feet from the stick and holed it. My worst, well...there was the time I went into the left fairway bunker, hit into the right trees, hit a low shot into the left bunker, wasted a shot in there, and took a quiet 8 with a 3-putter! Other times, I topped my second shot, or I went into the trees, or into the right hand fairway bunker! One time, come to think of it, I got a par when I hit a badly thinned drive. It was short of the fairway bunker, but it at least went straight. From there, I hit a 5-iron slightly right of the green. The ball was in light rough, and I chipped and 1-putted for par."

With this type of thinking, the plan is starting to come to-gether. The only way you got a birdie was by hitting a career drive, a career 9-iron from a downhill lie—a difficult shot for anybody—and then holing a six-footer. You've topped that downhill second shot many times! Any time you were in the trees or bunkers, you did badly. However, you got a nice par by unintentionally laying up short of the fairway bunkers, and all the tree trouble, and leaving your ball on a level lie.

You should lay up every time! Instead of taking a driver off the tee, take a fairway wood and lay up in the flat area short of the trouble. From there, it's just a 5-iron into the green from a good, level lie. You don't want to miss the shot left or short right, but if you favor the right side of the green and take enough club to carry the right bunker, you'll either make par or at worst a bogey, if you miss the green.

Continue to play each hole on your course in this way. You'll discover, perhaps, that it's wiser to lay up short of the green on that long par 4 guarded in front by bunkers—maybe the only times you've recently made par have been when you slightly mishit your second and chipped and 1-putted it. If there's water to the left off the tee of a narrow par 4, maybe you'll decide it's best for you to play for the right rough, which is never very heavy. There might be another hole, a par 5, where you face a big carry over water on your second shot, but where, even if you carry it, you're still sixty yards short of the green. You may conclude it's better to lay up short of the water and hit a medium iron in to the back of the green. When you've finished, you'll have come up with a pretty good plan, one you have a realistic chance of executing time after time.

One point particularly important for seniors is that your plan must reflect your current game, not the game you may have played as a youngster. To do this, make a point of learning how far you hit each club in your bag—*now*. I would discourage you from trying to pace off the length of your shots on the practice ground. First, if your practice ground is busy, it's not feasible. Second, at most courses you're no longer allowed to use a shag bag, and often the practice balls provided are so worn, you'd get little idea of your correct distances. What I am going to suggest is very simple. The next time you play a good shot with any club, note where it lands, and pace off the distance. What you want to know is your carry, not the carry and roll. This is because, when you want to carry a hazard, the roll won't help you! If you keep notes of these distances, you'll soon get a good idea of what you can realistically expect from each club.

Yardage is something we pros talk about all the time, but I've barely ever heard the word from a senior's lips! Yet, if there's one "secret" of the professional's success, it's knowing the yardage. It never ceases to amaze me how, in pro-ams, I know the yardages better than some of my partners, who play the course all the time. There's really no excuse for not knowing the yardage on your home course.

---

**Seniors: You must plan your strategy with the game you have now—not the one you had as a youngster. That means pacing off the carry you get with every club in your bag. Once you know that, you can plan intelligently.**

On par 4s, choose a convenient landmark such as a tree or sprinkler head close to where your tee shot generally finishes. Then pace off the yardage from there to the front, middle, and back of the green. On par 5s, pace off the yardage from the area where your second shot usually lands. There's no need to pace off any earlier, because in most cases you'll need two good woods. The only exception to this would be if you have to lay up in front of a water hazard or other problem area. On par 3s, if you have permanent markers that give accurate yardage to the middle of the green, all you have to do is pace off the distance from the front of the green to the middle and from the middle to the back. When you play the hole, pace off from the tee marker to the permanent marker and add or subtract that yardage from the total yardage. If you don't have such markers, then step off the yardage from the back of the tee to the front, middle and back of the green. Then, if the tee is placed forward, all you have to do is pace off the yardage from the back of the tee to the tee marker and subtract this figure from the total yardage.

## PLAN EACH SHOT

EARLIER, I talked about a physical routine before every shot, a step-by-step procedure designed to get you set up correctly every time. There's a mental side to this routine that is equally important.

Most of this mental routine takes place before you pick a club out of the bag. As an example, let's trace it, one step at a time, on an approach shot.

The first thing you must consider is your lie. You may normally have several different ways in which you could play a shot, but if the lie is poor, it may eliminate all but one of them. Having checked the lie, get the yardage and make a preliminary selection of club. Say it's 150 yards, for example, and you take a 6-iron from that distance. Then, you must consider the wind and weather conditions. For example, if the air is damp and heavy and the wind's against you, you'll have to go to a stronger club. You must also look at the target area, in this case, the green. Look at the hazards, and decide the best place to put the ball. For example, is the pin tucked behind a bunker? Perhaps you should play for the fat of the green? Does the green slope from right to left so that you should land on the right side and let the ball roll to the pin? And so on. A very important factor through all these considerations is your own skill level and also how you're playing. It's no good thinking of drawing the ball into the pin from the middle of the green if all you ever hit is a fade. Even if you can normally hit the draw, don't pick it on days when the shot is not working for you. You have to think of the best percentage shot on that day.

Here I should interject precisely what I mean by playing the percentages. As you visualize playing one type of shot or another, you should estimate how many times out of ten you can hit it successfully. Be very realistic in making this estimate. Then compare it with your estimates for the other shots you're exploring. The decision then practically makes itself. If, for example, you can only make one shot three times out of ten and another, seven times out of ten, go with the latter every time. That's exactly what we professionals do ninety-nine times out of a hundred, and that's one reason why we make far fewer "big numbers" on holes than you do.

At any rate, from all these considerations, you'll be starting to form mental pictures of possible shots and eventually you'll settle on your best shot in the circumstances. Once you've picked the shot you want to hit, then picture it clearly in your mind. Run it through your mind as you take your practice swings. Jack Nicklaus has described the process as like going to the movies. That's exactly right. You must imagine the feel of the right swing and in your mind's eye, see the ball flying to your target. Then step up to the ball and make the same swing without further ado. You want to make the shot while those mental images are clear and vivid.

## DON'T BE FOOLISH

ALTHOUGH I could probably write a whole book on foolish mistakes I've seen seniors make, I'll restrict myself to some of the more glaring ones.

First and foremost, so many seniors almost refuse to use their handicap intelligently. In boxing, there are no handicaps, no "free swings" at the champ, but in golf, if you lose some of your ability, you get more strokes in handicap. You must use this handicap intelligently. If you lose one stroke on a hole, don't allow it to upset you to the point where you lose three more in a hurry. Be philosophical about your mistakes, and just try to keep them to one at a time. Keep a tidy card! No eights, nines and tens, please.

If you play intelligently, you can win many matches off your handicap. For example, back home I often play against a friend, Fardel Allem, who's a nine handicapper. Both of us are farmers and our usual bet is a bale of hay, a cow, or something of that kind. Now I have to play him at plus three, so he gets twelve strokes. If he's thinking well, if he recovers well, and lays his long putts close, I'm in trouble!

Your main objective is to keep the ball in the fairway. If you hit into trouble, say, into a stand of trees, make certain you pick a shot that will definitely get you out in one stroke. Avoid "near-impossible" shots like the plague. We professionals sometimes have to hit them, and in exceptional circumstances, you might have to try to hit one, too. However, in your case, I would reserve that for the time when you're going to lose the entire match, not just a hole. So many times in amateur play, the player who chips out of trouble still gets a half because his opponent makes an unexpected mistake. Remember: He's not perfect either!

If there's severe trouble on one side of the hole—say, an out of bounds—then you must guard against it. If the out of bounds is on the left, never set up the ball with the clubface closed. You're asking for a pull or hook right into the trouble. In fact, if you're not playing well, even open the clubface a fraction before taking your grip—at least you know you'll miss on the right side. Similarly, if the out of bounds is on the right, slightly toeing the clubface in, closing it a little, will ensure you'll move the ball away from the trouble.

Take enough club! If I've said this once to my pro-am partners, I must have said it a thousand times. Most amateurs, but seniors particularly, are guilty of underclubbing to the point of insanity. Sometimes, of course, it's because they've got no idea how far they hit each club or the yardage. However, other times, it's sillier than that. For example, just because

---

**Seniors: Play your shot, not someone else's. If you know you should lay up short of a water hazard, ignore the fact that others are trying to carry it. Stick to your guns and lay up. Often, you'll have the last laugh!**

**Seniors: The older you get, the more you tend to think of ways to miss a shot than ways to make it. You try to steer the ball or even hit it so timidly, the shot has no chance of success. "Faint heart ne'er won fair lady" applies in golf just as much as it does in the game of love.**

everyone else in the group is taking an iron into a par 3 is no reason for you to take one, too. If your best way of playing the shot is an easy 5- or 7-wood, for example, then for goodness sake take it. There's no excuse for taking a long iron and leaving it halfway to the green. Never let your pride stand in the way of bringing off a successful shot! Always make it a rule to play for the back of the green. Then, if you mishit, you'll be in the middle. Most trouble is in front of the green.

The British have an expression for it that I like: Have a go! I think that seniors miss more shots because they're tentative than for any other reason. As you get older, you start recalling too many of the bad shots you've made in particular situations. As a result, you don't make a full-blooded, accelerating swing through the ball on full shots, or play your shots crisply around and on the green.

I remember that before the 1966 British Open I was very dissatisfied with my ball striking. I had spotted that my finish seemed very low, but otherwise I couldn't figure out what was wrong. I asked Ian Marchbanks, the Gleneagles (Scotland) professional, to have a look at my swing. He said one word to me: *Accelerate.* What a difference! Once I accelerated through the ball, I started striking the ball well again, getting good extension and finishing high. I was very thankful for Ian's advice, because by not going through the ball freely and fast, you can start to slice the ball, hook it, or even shank it!

So, make a habit of remembering your good shots in various situations. Then, you'll never get tentative and take a "powder-puff" swing or let the club "drop" on the ball.

*Remember: You must always accelerate the club through the ball.*

## DON'T LEAVE IT TO CHANCE

IF you get a good tip, one that really works for you, don't rely on your memory. The professional way is to keep a notebook, and make a note of it. Organize these notes under topics, such as grip, address, swing, irons, woods, short game, and so on, so that you can retrieve them when that portion of your game goes sour. If you have a personal computer, then by all means use it to store your notes.

Another thing you can do is to write yourself a reminder on the back of your glove. I did this when I won the U.S. Open in 1965. I wrote 'SLOW' on the back of my glove so that on every shot I was reminded to swing slow. If I'm not too proud to do this, then you shouldn't be either!

## CHAPTER EIGHT

# *PROBLEM SHOTS MADE EASY*

THERE'S NO DOUBT IN MY MIND that one of the hardest things in golf for most seniors is to hit the ball successfully from problem lies or under difficult conditions. However, I think your problem is not so much your golfing ability. It's simply that you've never learned the correct techniques to cope with these circumstances.

I quite understand how frustrating it must be for you, for example, to thin or top the ball whenever you have a downhill lie. However, I assure you that, once you know what you should do in each case, you'll start enjoying some success. Then, I think you'll relish the challenge presented by such problem shots.

If you think about it, golf would be a pretty dull game if every shot were played from a flat tee or a flat, perfect fairway lie and always under the same perfect conditions!

However, I must admit that when I saw one lie I had when coming down the stretch in the 1987 Mazda Senior Tournament Players Championship, it made me devoutly wish I had put the ball on a flat piece of grass! At the thirteenth hole, I drove in the right side of the fairway onto quite a severe slope. I was 140 yards from the pin, which was tucked behind a bunker on the right of the green. The ball was well above my feet, and this lie normally makes you hook. Yet, I had to fade the ball, because the wind was blowing from right to left and I also had to avoid hitting some trees on the right! I gripped my 7-iron very short, took it way outside the line, and hit it firmly. The ball carried the bunker by no more than six inches and finished two feet from the hole, and I holed the putt for a birdie.

Although it's hard to say that a single shot won a championship, that 7-iron will linger long in my memory because, in order to get the ball close, I had to break number 3 of my own "rules" for sloping lies (below). I would hasten to add that it is one thing for a Senior Tour professional to try this shot in an attempt to win a major, and quite another for a senior weekender in a casual game! That was about as good a shot as I can hit!

I urge you to practice the techniques that follow. Ben Hogan once said, "Never play a shot you haven't practiced recently." That's very true. However, some shots you can simply choose not to play. The shots that follow are ones that *all* of us have to play. So, be prepared!

## SLOPING LIES

FROM my observation in pro-ams, most of you seniors have a problem with sloping lies because you *fight* the slopes instead of adapting to them. With a ball-above-feet lie, for example, you try to prevent the ball from flying from right to left, and do exactly the opposite on a lie with the ball below the feet. On an uphill lie, you try to keep the ball low and end up hitting into the hill. On a downhill lie, you try to help the ball up; you "scoop" it up with a flick of the right hand, and top it.

Instead, you must realize that there are what I call five "golden rules" to playing off slopes. Here they are.

*Rule 1. Whichever way the ground slopes, that is the direction in which the ball will fly.*

When the ball is above your feet, the ball will fly from right to left. If the ball is below your feet, it will fly from left to right. If you have an uphill lie, the ball will fly higher than usual, a downhill lie, lower.

*Rule 2. Whichever way the ground slopes, that is the direction in which you tend to "fall."*

With the ball above your feet, if you're going to lose your balance, it usually will be backward; with the ball below your feet, forward. Off an uphill lie, you tend to fall back to your right; on a downhill lie, to your left. As you'll see, these tendencies dictate how you should balance your weight at address.

*Rule 3. Make your regular swing.*

As I said earlier, don't fight the slope by changing your swing. Don't try to swing out to in to fade the ball on ball-above-feet-lies, or more in to out to hook it in on ball-below-feet lies. Unless you're highly skilled, such maneuvers usually end in a complete miss. The same thinking applies to uphill and downhill lies. Instead, make your normal swing, and let the ball's flight follow the dictates of the slope.

*Rule 4. Swing more easily than usual.*

On sloping lies, it's very difficult to keep your balance. You must remember that. The harder you swing at the ball, the more likely you are to lose your balance, and mess up the shot. On more severe slopes, you may well have to cut back on the length of your backswing to keep your balance.

*Rule 5. Stay centered and get the club through the ball.*

I've seen many of you seniors who make the mistake of pulling yourselves off the ball during the swing. As a result, you quit on the shot. To counteract this, work on keeping the body and especially the head very steady. Also, you must make certain you hit the ball first, something that is nearly impossible to do if you're off balance.

On extremely severe slopes, it's a good idea to keep the lower body still and play the shot more with the hands and arms. The way to learn that is to use the "feet together" drill described in Chapter Four; it will help you develop exactly the right action.

Generally, the only changes you should make to cope with sloping lies are at address. These changes, which we'll now discuss, are designed to accommodate your address to the particular slope so that you can make as natural a swing as is possible in the circumstances.

**Ball above feet.** Whatever you do at address from a ball-above-feet lie, the ball will fly from right to left. So the first adjustment is to aim right of target—the more severe the slope, the more severe the hook you'll get and the more you should aim to the right.

The basic problem on these lies is that you're forced to stand more erect than normal. Such a posture will force you to swing on a flatter plane and hook the ball. To minimize this tendency, go to a stronger club than the one you'd normally use from that

CHOKE DOWN ON CLUB

WEIGHT ON BALLS OF FEET

*With the ball above the feet, you swing flatter and draw the ball.*

distance, and choke well down on the handle. On extreme ball-above-feet lies, your right index finger can be close to or even on the steel. Also, put more weight on the balls of your feet than the heels and stand closer to the ball.

There's another reason for choking down on a stronger club. If you took a big swing from this type of lie, you're going to get a very big hook. If you know you have more than enough club in your hand, you'll tend to swing easier. This minimizes the hook, and allows you to keep your balance and make a solid strike.

Be very careful how you set the blade at address. If you inadvertently set it closed (facing left of your intended swing line), the combination of a flatter swing and closed clubface will give the worst hook you've ever seen. As a "safety" measure, I suggest you set the blade slightly open (facing right of your intended swing line), then weaken the left hand a little (turn it left) before taking your grip.

**Ball below feet.** Despite the adjustments you make at address, the ball is still going to fly from left to right from a ball-below-feet lie. So, the first thing to do is aim left of target to allow for it.

HOLD CLUB
AT END

WEIGHT
ON HEELS

*With the ball below the feet,
you swing more upright and
fade the ball.*

On this lie, the basic problem is that you're forced to lean over the ball more than normal. This in turn sets up a more upright swing and a slice. Unlike the other sloping lies, where choking down on the club is either necessary or helpful, you should never choke down on a ball-below-feet lie. If you did, you'd be doubled over at address. No one—including myself —could make a good swing from such an uncomfortable posture. Instead, you should hold the club at the end of the handle and bring the hands very close to the body. Then you can stand slightly more erect, in a more normal posture. Position the weight more toward the heels.

You should definitely go to a stronger club. If you had a 7-iron shot off such a lie, the ideal club would be a 7-iron with a shaft that was six inches longer than usual. Since you don't have such a club in your bag, go with the stronger club like a 6-iron or even a 5-iron, if the lie is severe. Then, as always on sloping lies, swing easier.

When the ball is below your feet, be careful how you set the blade at address. Never, but never, position it open. Instead, as a safety measure, set the blade a little bit closed, and strengthen the grip of the left hand—turn it right a bit—before gripping the handle.

**Uphill.** On uphill lies, you must compensate for the higher flight of the ball by choosing a less lofted club than you'd normally take for the distance. Play the ball back a bit in your stance, and make certain your hands are a little ahead of the ball.

The tendency on this shot is to put too much weight on the right foot, and position the left shoulder too high and have the hands behind the ball. This combination increases the effective loft of the club and when you hit up on the ball so much it flies far too high.

To get the body in a more normal position, bend the left knee a little more than usual. You can't avoid having somewhat more weight on the right foot, because if you put all your weight on the left foot, you would merely drive the ball into the slope. You must have enough weight on the right foot so that you can swing through up the slope and get the ball airborne. However, because the weight will favor the right foot, it does become difficult to shift your weight to the left foot on the downswing. As a result, the left hip clears or turns to the left faster than usual, which in turn causes the hands to release a little sooner, and you'll draw the ball. It's a good idea to allow for this by aiming a little to the right of the target.

*On an uphill lie, flex the left knee more ball flies high and draws.*

**Downhill.** On a downhill lie, you must compensate for the ball flying lower by taking a more lofted club than usual. To avoid hitting the ground behind the ball, play the ball back in your stance, with the hands ahead of the ball. If you play the ball in the normal position in the stance, a common mistake, you'll hit the ground behind the ball in the takeaway.

Your goal on downhill lies is to make the clubhead path through the ball match the slope. However, don't make the mistake of putting too much weight on the left foot. Do that, and your left shoulder is so low that you hit down on the ball too much, and never get it up. Instead, bend the right knee more than usual so that the shoulders aren't tilted as much and the body is more vertical.

The downhill lie is the only exception to the rule that you shouldn't change your basic swing on sloping lies. You obviously can't take your normal "one piece" takeaway, sweeping the ball back, because, if you do, you'll hit the slope. To clear it, start cocking the wrists immediately as you start the club back.

Despite your best efforts to stay centered, the tendency is for the slope to pull you to the left on the downswing. Your body slides a little past the ball, and this prevents your hands from

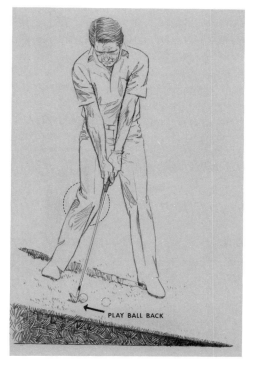

*On a downhill lie, flex the right knee more. The ball flies low and fades.*

PLAY BALL BACK

> **Seniors: On sloping lies, too many of you put too much body into the shot, lose your balance, and mishit the ball. Remember: The more severe the slope, the more you must keep the head still and hit the ball with your hands and arms.**

fully releasing. You tend to leave the clubface a little open at impact, and fade the ball. Allow for this tendency by aiming a little left of target.

## IN THE ROUGH

IN playing from rough, you must consider your lie, really study it, before making any sort of decision on club selection. The worst thing you can do is select a club based on the distance you need and then go into the rough and try to make it work. You have to decide what club is possible from the lie— can you hit a wood, a medium iron, or is it so bad that you need a short iron or even your sand wedge? Answer these questions first, then worry about your yardage, the conditions, the target area, and so on.

If the rough is not severe, and you need distance, then by all means use a well lofted wood like a 5- or 7-wood. You'll find that a wood will slip through the grass far more easily than an iron. If you don't have a 5- or 7-wood, but, say, only a 4-wood, you can get good results by opening the face of the club before taking your grip, aiming a little left of target and playing for a fade. Remember to use a weaker grip than usual in playing this shot.

> **Seniors: Clint Eastwood said it best—"A man has to know his limitations." If you have a poor lie, play the shot you know you can make successfully. Don't attempt the shot you would have played if you had put the ball on a perfect lie.**

*In rough, grip firmly, play the ball back, and make a more upright swing.*

If the lie is not so favorable and you need to play an iron, then grip just a little firmer than usual to prevent the club turning in the hands. Your prime objective is to put the club on the ball with as little grass getting between the clubface and the ball as possible. Don't attempt to sweep the club back—you'll catch too much grass. Instead, play the ball farther back in the stance, the hands ahead of the ball, and pick the club up more sharply than usual, breaking the wrists immediately in the takeaway. This will give you a more upright swing so you can hit down steeply. Whatever you do, don't quit at the ball. Try to swing through into as full a follow-through as you can. If you're playing a 7-iron or more lofted club, keep most of your weight on the left foot. With less lofted irons, use normal weight distribution.

If you encounter severe rough, it can catch the clubhead and turn the clubface left at impact, sending the ball left. It's a good idea, therefore, to open the stance and aim a little right of target in the circumstances.

Seniors must realize their limitations in heavy rough. It's one of those occasions when you remember how you used to play the shot, rather than what is realistic now. If you have lost a little strength, be aware of it and, if anything, take one more lofted club than you think is necessary.

*In severe rough, aim the blade a little right, and open the stance.*

Another good reason for taking a more lofted club is that, try as you may to hit cleanly on the back of the ball, you'll usually catch some grass behind the ball, and the ball will "fly" on you. What happens is that the grass acts as a lubricant, and instead of getting your usual amount of backspin, the ball flies out with very little spin, often carrying and rolling much farther than usual.

A most important point is you never know exactly how the ball is going to react from medium or heavy rough. So, you should never expect pinpoint accuracy. If the pin is tucked behind a bunker, for example, this is not the time to fire right at it. Instead, give yourself as big a margin for error as you can and hit for the middle of the green.

If you get into really long grass, take your medicine and hit out safely with your sand wedge. Open the stance, open the blade and play the shot much like a regular bunker shot. Keep your cool at all costs. Take a deep breath, let it out, and relax. Then calmly select a target for your recovery that will set up your next shot. It's all too easy to get a little "hot," and that's the time you'll hit from the right rough straight into the left rough!

## OTHER PROBLEM LIES

**Divot holes.** Occasionally, your ball will finish in an old divot hole. This shot is rarely as tough as many seniors make it. What makes it tough is a poor attitude, saying to yourself something like, "This is unfair. I hit the ball right down the middle of the fairway, and now look at the lie I have!" Then, you're liable to grab the wood or iron you were planning to use oblivious of the lie, and dub the shot. Come on, now, you're old enough to know better than that!

*From a divot hole, take a well lofted club, and play the ball back.*

Instead, treat the divot hole shot in the same way you would one from the rough. In other words, the lie determines what club you can use.

To play the shot, position the ball back in your stance—the deeper the divot hole, the farther you put it back. You should take a more lofted club than normal, because by playing the ball back, you reduce the club's effective loft. Generally, never take a less lofted club than a 5-iron on this shot. Going back, break your wrists quickly, taking the club up more steeply, and hit down sharply on the ball. You should keep your left hand pulling all the way through on this shot so that the hands are well in advance of the clubhead at impact. I like to feel as though I'm hitting the ball very cleanly, almost thinning it. This seems to give me the best results.

**Hardpan.** If your ball comes to rest on hardpan, a hard piece of bare ground, then you can play the shot similarly to a divot hole—position the ball a little back in the stance, make a quicker wrist break, and hit down more steeply on the ball.

*From hardpan, play the ball back, and hit down steeply on the ball.*

However, for more skilled players, there is another way to play it, with a fade. Aim slightly left of target, align your feet and shoulders to the left on a line parallel to the aim, and take a weaker grip. The slightly out to in swing you will get leads to a steeper descent on the ball and you'll get it up very easily.

**Perched Lie.** Sometimes, your ball will come to rest on the top of some thick grass so that it is perched high off the ground. Most seniors love this type of lie, but it's surprising how often they go right underneath the ball, skying the ball up in the air. This usually comes from pressing the club down in the grass behind the ball. However, it can also be caused by hitting down on the ball too steeply. What you want to do is to choke down on the club a little so that, at address, the clubface is directly behind the ball, at ball level. Then work on a good one piece backswing and a sweeping type of hit.

Even if you're hitting an iron, imagine that you're using a wood, and you'll get the right sort of swing.

*With a perched lie, choke down and use a sweeping swing.*

## WIND AND WET

ON windy or wet days, the first adjustment you should make is a mental one. You simply are not going to score quite as well as in perfect conditions. Once you accept that, and realize that the weather is the same for everyone, you're halfway toward playing well in bad conditions. You need patience in golf any time, but on a wet or windy day you need a double dose of it. You're probably going to miss more shots than usual, and you're going to have to keep a tight rein on your temper, but, if you do, you're going to beat a lot of people, including many of the youngsters!

The basic skill needed on a windy day is to keep the ball down. Up high, the ball is at the mercy of the wind, but down low, it seldom comes to much harm. What you have to remember is a basic equation: The harder you hit the ball, the more backspin you put on it, and the higher it flies. Conversely, if you hit it easier, you put less backspin on it and it will fly lower, out of harm's way. So, instead of hitting your normal 7-iron for a certain distance, take a 5-iron, choke down on it, and try to hit it the same distance you would a 7-iron. By taking a more straight-faced club, and swinging easier, you'll keep the ball down.

Against the wind, it's especially important to think of swinging easier. All your instincts tell you to hit harder, but resist them. A head wind will increase any backspin you put on the ball, and, even if you swing at your normal swing speed, it can easily get up too high. If you hit hard, it's a case of "gone with the wind!" With a driver, don't tee the ball low. You're liable to hit down too steeply, put too much backspin on the ball, and get it up too high. On approach shots, remember that the ball will stop more quickly on the green—you must take enough club to allow for this. If you have to carry a bunker, play for the back of the green. Then, if you inadvertently hit the ball too high, you'll still carry the bunker.

It's worth adding that a Surlyn ball is marvellous on a windy day. The wind has far less effect on it than on a balata ball.

As a general rule, don't try to be clever in crosswinds, and "hold" the ball in the wind with a fade or draw. Just aim to the left or right of target and let the wind bring the ball back. However, if your natural shape of shot is a draw or fade, then you're going to be "holding" the ball half the time anyway. If you draw the ball, and you have a left-to-right wind, your draw will hold the ball straight. Similarly, if you fade the ball in a right-to-left wind, your fade will hold the ball straight. In both cases, remember that you're going to lose some distance, so take one or two clubs stronger than usual, depending on the strength of the wind.

If you do have the skill to move the ball both ways, then that's a different matter. Off the tee, you have two options. If you want an extra long ball, and the hole is relatively open, then "ride" the wind by aiming a little left of target in a left-to-right wind and fading the ball. In a right-to-left wind, aim a little right and draw the ball. However, if the hole is tight or you're playing into a green, then "holding" the ball into the wind is usually the best option. It gives you the most control, because the spin fights the wind and drops the ball dead on the ground.

Downwind shots are in many ways the most difficult. The wind will take backspin off the ball, "knocking it down," as we say on tour. On tee shots don't try to overpower the ball, but take a normal, full swing—you want as much backspin as you can get. In a really stiff wind, say twenty-five to thirty miles an hour, it will pay you to use a 3-wood off the tee to get the ball up in the air. On approach shots, play a low, running shot whenever you can. Play the ball back in your stance a bit, and "punch" it with firm hands and wrists. Then, you don't have to worry about the wind knocking the ball down. My colleague

**Seniors: Never trust your instincts in a wind—They tell you to hit hard into the wind, and softly downwind. You should do exactly the opposite!**

on the Senior Tour, Doug Sanders, has that shot down pat. Study him closely, if you get the chance. However, if you have a bunker or other hazard between you and the green, you have to play a shot with a normal trajectory. Then, it's best to take the weakest club that will give you the distance when struck firmly. Even then, the shot is difficult to control.

On wet days, the air is heavy, and once the ground gets soggy, you won't get much roll. With a driver, you want to keep the ball in the air as long as possible, so tee the ball a bit higher than usual. On iron shots, look at the front of the ball, not the back. Then, if anything, you'll thin the ball a little. *You must not hit the ball fat!* If you do, you'll regret it. With all that wet grass and earth getting between the clubface and the ball at impact, the ball can squirt off anywhere. As a general rule, take two clubs more than you would normally. You must get the ball to the hole. Write that on your glove on a rainy day!

If you have the misfortune to go into the rough, remember that wet grass is particularly difficult. You must take a much more lofted club than on a dry day. Another reason for a more lofted club is that's it's difficult to put backspin on a ball from wet rough. With too little loft, you won't get the ball up and out of there.

A wet day contradicts one of the fundamental rules of chipping. Normally, it's best to take the lowest lofted club that will get you a yard or so onto the green and then let the ball roll to the hole. When it's wet, it becomes difficult to judge roll, so take a more lofted club and carry the ball most of the way to the hole. You'll find this a far more dependable method than trying to run the ball through water. When putting, hit the ball firmly and play for less break than you'd normally take.

## CHAPTER NINE

# *TURN TRAP SHOTS INTO SAND PLAY*

**M**OST SENIORS, I've noticed, don't call a bunker a "bunker;" they use the word *trap*. Now, there's a negative word if ever I heard one! This is because playing from a bunker is probably the shot they fear most. If I do nothing else for you in this chapter, I hope I can help you overcome this fear and remove the word "trap" from your vocabulary once and for all!

If you've never learned how to play from bunkers, and most seniors haven't, then you should realize that being a poor sand player is not merely a matter of having a chink in your golfing armor. It permeates your whole game. On approach shots, greenside bunkers can intimidate you to the point of pulling or pushing your irons off line in a frantic attempt not to "get trapped." Off the tee, the sight of a fairway bunker often does exactly the same thing.

In contrast, if you finally learn to master the sand, it will give a lift to your whole game. You'll swing freely on your long shots and approach shots alike, and as we've discussed, a free swing, where you trust centrifugal force to do the job for you on the downswing, is the best swing. You'll also find you can attack the course, because you *know* you can recover from a bunker.

There's no question in my mind that my sand play has largely been responsible for my winning nine major championships. I can't tell you the number of times it's helped me play an aggressive shot when I needed it, or, when I've missed the green, I've been able to knock the ball out a foot or so from the hole, and turn what seemed like a sure bogey into an easy par.

My most memorable bunker shot had to be the one at the seventy-second hole of the 1961 Masters. I had taken a four-stroke lead over Arnold Palmer into the last round, and was still three strokes ahead after the first nine holes, which I shot in 34. Then, things started to go wrong. To cut a long story short, on the eighteenth hole, I hit my 4-iron second shot into the right-hand bunker. I was pin high, and the flag was down at the bottom of the green, the ground between the bunker and hole sloping downhill away from me. Not the easiest of shots. However, I managed to put the ball four feet from the hole and holed the putt. I had shot 40 on the back nine, and out on the fifteenth, Arnold now had a one-stroke lead.

When Arnold came to the eighteenth, all he needed was a par for victory. I was watching on TV. He hit a great drive, and only had a 7-iron into the green. He faded the shot a little and it finished in a slightly buried lie in the same bunker I had visited earlier. What happened next I could scarcely believe. Arnold, I saw, was playing the buried lie with a wide open blade! Bobby Jones, who was with me, noticed this also, and said, "He should square the face, and 'pop' it out." Sure enough, Arnold hit a poor shot, and skulled the ball across the green and down a slope. He then played a Texas wedge that finished fifteen feet away and missed the putt.

It took a moment for everything to sink in. I realized I had won! I was so happy, I could have jumped ten feet in the air, yet at the same time I was sad for Arnold, losing because of such an unaccountable mental lapse. I also realized the significance of my own bunker shot on the eighteenth. If I had given up on the shot, golf's history book might well have recorded a different winner.

Of course, even the best sand players need a little luck now and then. My luckiest shot was one I hit at the twelfth hole at Augusta in 1965, the year Arnold and I finished second to Jack Nicklaus. The flag was on the back right-hand corner of the green, which was very hard and firm. Even if one had had a good lie in the bunker, he would have had a tough job to keep the ball on the green. What I had done was to bury my ball under the back lip! I could only see the ball from the bottom of the bunker. When I took my address, the lip hid the ball from sight. I considered declaring it unplayable, but eventually elected to chop down through the lip. All I was looking for was to duff the ball into the bottom of the bunker so that I would get a decent lie. I hit down on the ball. It pitched in the bunker once, twice, came out, hit the flag, and went right into the hole!

Although you'll get your share of "lucky" shots, too, I can't impress on you enough that basically good sand play comes down to two things: First, knowing the right techniques, and second, practicing them. As I've said many times, the harder I practice, the luckier I seem to get! Also, the better you learn to play from sand, the less you'll think of "having to get out of those so and so traps!" Instead, you'll think of bunkers and "sand play."

"Sand play" was fun when you were a kid. It can be again, if you have the knowledge and then apply it.

## GREENSIDE BUNKERS

IF you study the great sand players, it appears there must be hundreds of different ways to play the greenside bunker shot. Sam Snead plays them with a long, slow, swing. Julius Boros plays them with such a loose swing, it almost looks sloppy. In contrast, Chi Chi Rodriguez plays them more quickly, firmly. Then there's Isao Aoki, the great Japanese player—he almost chops the ball out. There's no consistency, right?

Wrong! What these great players are doing is to play their sand shots with the same type of swing they use in their long game. That, by itself, is one of the secrets of becoming a successful sand player.

So many of you seniors have been misled by instruction that implies that you must somehow change your swing completely once you step into a bunker. You try to "take" the club back away from the body to the outside or pull the arms violently across the ball. That's not the way to go. You don't have to make drastic changes in your swing to play the sand well. You don't have to change your natural swing plane or the feel of your normal swing. Most of the changes are made at address. Then, you go ahead and swing normally.

Your overall approach to greenside bunkers should be the

Seniors: On greenside bunker shots, don't just try to put the ball "somewhere" on the green—that's all you'll do. Instead, try to hole them. You'll put the ball far closer, or even hole it out!

same as any other short game shot. *You aim to hole it!* If this sounds ridiculous, consider this. If you were putting from twenty feet, you'd try to hole it. If you were chipping from twenty feet, you'd try to hole it. Now, why would you want to change your goals just because the ball is lying in sand?

I can hear you saying, "That's not for me. I'd be happy just getting the ball out of the trap."

I've got news for you, my friend, that's old-fashioned thinking!

When I was a young man, that's all that many pretty good golfers tried to do. If they were ambitious, they tried to "get the ball close." I soon realized that even "close" was not good enough. This is because your mind and body respond to the target area as perceived by your eyes. If you merely try to get out somewhere, that's all you'll do. If you try to get close, that mental image is a little sharper—say, a circle ten or fifteen feet in diameter around the hole—and you'll probably succeed in putting the ball somewhere in that circle. However, if you try to hole the shot, you'll finish closer to the hole than with any other target in mind, and you're going to get your share of hole-outs, too!

I realized that I was on the right track when I was playing in the 1958 World Cup at Kasumigaseki, Japan. I noticed that the two Japanese players, Torakichi Nakamura and Koichi Ono, asked their caddies to take the flagstick out of the hole every time they went into a greenside bunker. They, too, were aiming to hole out! Believe me, they came so close to doing this every time, it was unbelievable. Incidentally, Japan won the team event that year, with Nakamura defeating me for the International Trophy, 274–281.

Trying to hole out the ball triggers the same type of thinking as on a putt or a chip, and correctly so. When you have a putt, you determine whether you should aim left or right because of a break, whether you're playing up or downhill, whether the grass is long or short, whether it's dry or wet, whether you're playing into the grain (slower), downgrain (faster) or cross grain, and so on. *You should do exactly the same thing on a bunker shot.* Check all these conditions, then determine the spot where you want the ball to land, visualize the right swing and the ball landing on that spot and then rolling *into the hole*.

When I was a young man, I used to get up at six o'clock and practice sand shots for two hours before I went to breakfast. Later, as I improved, I made a point of holing five sand shots before I quit. This may sound a little much for you right now, but promise me you'll *try* to hole every sand shot you hit. I guarantee that you'll improve.

You also, of course, must train yourself to read the sand. Very often the average senior doesn't realize that the type of lie determines the shot you must play. If you're in a buried lie, for example, you can't put backspin on the ball, you'll always get some roll. If the ball is slightly buried, the ball won't run as much as when completely buried. If you're playing from very, very soft sand, the ball will come out slower; from wet sand, faster.

Another little known fact is that you get the maximum backspin when the sand is fairly firm, and rakes are not being used. What you do is attach a length of ordinary pipe to the end of a rake handle (in place of the rake) and scrape the bunkers with that. The Japanese came up with this idea, and Jack Nicklaus and I both try to incorporate this into our course designs. We believe that people want to see good bunker shots. If you make the sand all rough and soft, you're making it impossible for a man to recover. The way the officials "hide" the pins (behind bunkers) these days, you must give a man a chance to put it close. As Bobby Locke once told me, "You don't ask a good pool player to play on a poor table."

Besides the correct mental approach to the shot, you must also have the correct technique. So, let's get at it.

## FROM A GOOD LIE

BEFORE taking your stance in the sand, you should wriggle your feet down to get a firm stance. You can also get an idea of the sand's texture. To compensate for the lower position of your feet, and for better control, choke down a little on the sand wedge.

On virtually every greenside bunker shot from a good lie, I set my body—feet, hips and shoulders—in an open position so that imaginary lines across them would point to the left of target. I also open the clubface, so that it faces right of target.

The swing follows the open body alignment—you swing back outside the line to the target, and through across it. So in effect, you're making a slice swing, putting cut on the ball. However, I repeat you don't feel as though you're making a completely different type of swing than normal. It's as though you were playing a wedge shot straight to the left of the hole. The open blade compensates for swinging across the ball, so that the ball flies about halfway between the line of swing and the direction in which the clubface is pointing.

I do recommend setting the weight a bit more on the left foot than the right. This will encourage you to break the wrists earlier than usual. An early set is important on a bunker shot—you must take the club up steeply enough to clear the sand. On the downswing, key on accelerating through the ball into a good, high, full finish.

The open blade also does one other thing for you that I must now explain. You might think that with the weight on the left foot, and a fairly steep downward hit, you would dig deeply into the sand. This is where the "bounce" on the sand wedge, described in Chapter Five, comes into play. By opening the blade, you increase the bounce, and compensate for the steep hit so that the club skids through the sand, taking a shallow cut, rather than digging in.

The two biggest mistakes I see seniors make in regard to the greenside sand shot are: 1. Not opening the face of the sand wedge enough. They set the blade square, and the club digs in too much, and 2. Using a club with a very narrow flange, one with no bounce and a sharp leading edge, or using a pitching wedge for the shot, which amounts to the same thing.

The modern shot is a "skid through" shot using a club with "bounce." Remember that.

The amount that you open the stance and blade depends on the length of the shot. The shorter the shot, the more you open the body and blade. The longer the shot, the less you open them.

For a very short shot, I open up so much that the body almost faces the hole and I use a very open blade. This creates more of an abrupt, up and down, more V-shaped swing arc which gets the ball up quickly. I play the ball up off the left heel and plan to enter the sand about an inch and a half behind

**Seniors: From a good lie in the sand, you must open the sand wedge. When the ball's buried, you must square the blade. I see more bad sand shots from seniors because they violate these rules than for any other reason.**

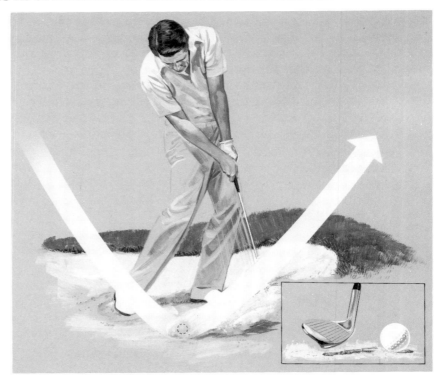

On a short sand shot, use a very open blade and stance, creating a steep,
V-shaped swing.

the ball. You must remember that with such an open body
alignment and blade, you're going to put a lot of cut (or slice
spin) on the ball. This means it will spin to the right on landing. You must take this sidespin into consideration when
you're picking your landing spot.

On shorter shots, I recommend using what I call an "early
flip" action. You flip the right hand under the left through impact. This action not only keeps the blade open through impact, it also increases the effective loft of the club, throwing
the ball up. Actually, what you do is to "hit from the top" a
little so that the clubhead reaches the ball slightly ahead of the
hands. There'll be a concave break in the back of the left wrist
at impact.

The way to get the feel of this is to go into a bunker, take a
ball in your right hand and toss it out underhand. Then try
hitting a ball from the same spot, using the same action. Alternate "throwing" and "hitting." You'll soon acquire the correct
feel.

On short shots, I believe in using a short swing. A long swing on a short shot leads to deceleration, which is fatal.

To play a slightly higher shot than usual, play the ball a bit more forward toward the left foot and set the weight on the right foot. Position the hands slightly behind the ball, setting up even more "early flip." Play this shot when the hole is just over the lip of the bunker.

On longer shots, the less open stance and blade gives you more of a U-shaped swing arc—there's a flatter bottom to the arc through the ball—which drives the ball more forward. On longer shots, put the ball back in the center of the stance and set the weight well forward on the left foot. On the downswing, you want to pull through strongly with the left hand ahead of the ball at impact. In effect, you hit extra late and

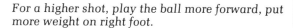

*For a higher shot, play the ball more forward, put more weight on right foot.*

On a long sand shot,
use a less open blade
and stance, creating a
more U-shaped swing.

there's a slightly convex position of the left wrist at impact. This action takes loft off the club so that you hit the ball lower.

On longer shots, take a longer swing. A short swing on a longer shot won't give you the necessary force to get the ball up to the hole. Also, aim to enter the sand closer to the ball; about three-quarters of an inch is about right. These adjustments give you a "skip and hold" action useful when the hole is at the back of the green, say, about a thirty-yarder.

I had just such a shot during the last round of the 1987 U.S. Senior Open. I was playing with Chi Chi Rodriguez, and at the sixth hole, which is about a drive and a 6-iron, I put my second shot far to the right into a bunker. It was a thirty-yarder, one of the toughest shots in the game, and, to complicate matters, the green sloped down and away from me with a right-to-left break. I put the ball one foot from the hole.

Chi Chi came over to me and said, "What a great shot! There's only one other man in the world who could have played it!" I replied, "And that's you, Chich!"

Seriously though, Chi Chi was absolutely right. I've never seen a finer sand player. If you get the chance to see him play these shots, you must take advantage of it. He has the greatest pair of hands in the golf business.

If you encounter wet sand, you must adjust the distance you

normally hit behind the ball. The clubhead won't cut so deeply into the sand as when the sand is dry. So you need to slow the clubhead speed by hitting farther behind the ball.

Seniors often play away from their home course, so the following can be very important to many of you. If you usually play a course where there is plenty of sand in the bunkers and one day you're playing from bunkers where there's little sand and what there is of it is hard, you must take a shorter swing back and through than you normally would. In other words, you must hit the shot a lot easier to allow for the club bouncing up a little off the sand, rather than skidding through it as usual. If you took your normal swing, the ball would come out too fast, and fly the green. The reverse applies if you normally play hard bunkers and visit a course whose bunkers have much more sand. You'll have to take a longer swing than usual to get the necessary force.

## ABNORMAL LIES

PROBABLY the lie most feared by seniors is the buried lie. They think they have to make a huge effort to get the ball out, and hit so hard they lose all control. Once you know what to do, you'll realize that it's not how hard you hit that matters, it's using the correct technique.

To play this lie successfully, you must *square* the blade at address. This negates the bounce on the wedge so that you cut down deeply into the sand under the ball. This is the one time you don't want an open blade, because then the sole will bounce off the sand into the back of the ball, which will often fly the green.

If you have a lot of green to work with, need to send the ball a fair distance, or the ball is in a "fried egg" lie (in the middle of a saucer-like depression in the sand), take a slightly open stance, play the ball back toward the right foot, and set the hands well ahead of the ball. (See the photos.) The weight should favor the left foot. This setup will help you break your wrists early, taking the club up steeply. Then hit down sharply, entering the sand about two inches behind the ball. Like any other sand shot, feel as though you're accelerating through. However, the resistance of the sand will cut off the finish much earlier than usual. Because of all the sand that gets be-

*On a buried lie, you must square the blade. Take a slightly open stance, with more weight on the left foot. Play the ball back, hands well ahead of the ball. Break your wrists early, taking the club up steeply. Then hit down sharply about two inches behind the ball.*

tween the blade and ball, you can't put spin on this shot—it will run when it hits the green.

If the pin is very close, just over the lip of the bunker, you could play the shot I've just described. However, the ball is obviously going to run far past the pin, leaving you a very long putt. If you have a "fried egg," you have no choice—you must enter the sand well behind the ball. However, let's say the ball is buried, but has buried itself in its own pitch mark. This means, of course, that the sand is fairly soft.

We get this shot on tour a lot these days because so many times new sand is dumped in the bunkers a short time before the tournament and so the sand has not had time to pack down. So, we've had to develop a variation of the shot described above to cope with the situation. Here's how to play it.

Square the blade and play the ball back in the middle of a fairly narrow, very open stance. Put practically all your weight on the left foot. These address adjustments will help you make the right type of swing, an abrupt up and down motion. Break the wrists very quickly and pick up the sand wedge at a very steep angle. Then, hit down as steeply as possible and as close to the ball as you can, cutting down deeply beneath it. You get

virtually no follow-through, leaving the clubhead in the sand just past the ball's original position.

The feel of the shot is much like making a soft karate chop on the ball. Have you ever put undercut on a table tennis ball? That's exactly the action you want. It's not a violent shot—swing too hard and you'll mess up. As always, use your normal swing tempo.

This technique gives you the softest shot possible in the circumstances. Because you've descended so steeply on the ball, the ball jumps up steeply, too. It won't have much spin, but it will fly high, drop softly on the green and won't have much roll.

Playing a putter from a bunker is considered a smart play by many of the senior golfers I've partnered. It is, but only if the conditions are right. You can consider using a putter if you're in a bunker fairly close to the green and the bunker has a low lip—no more than a few inches high. If you have a downhill lie and the sand is wet, hard, or both, then the putter often will be your best percentage shot. However, please don't try it from soft, fluffy sand—as so many of my pro-am teammates have demonstrated, it's too easy to duff the shot.

If you decide to play the putter, remember to take a long, careful look at all aspects of your intended line—the texture of the sand, the slope of the bunker up to the lip, the height of the lip, the length of grass on the lip and apron as well as the amount of green you have to putt over. This will help you get an idea of how much harder you must hit the ball than on a putt of similar length.

Most seniors come up short on this one, I've found, and I'm sure it's because they just go into the bunker and play the shot without paying attention to these details.

Don't ever attempt to chip from bunkers—it's far too risky. I've seen too many great players try it and leave the ball in the sand. Rarely will you leave the ball in the bunker if you use a regular sand wedge shot.

If you encounter a sidehill lie in a bunker, the techniques I described earlier apply. However, here are a few additional thoughts.

**Uphill.** If you take the same amount of sand as usual, you're liable to hit the shot too high and short. On a shot where you'd normally plan to enter the sand an inch and a half behind the ball, hit only an inch behind. Position your hands slightly ahead of the ball to help you hit through the upslope.

**Downhill.** From a downhill lie, it's all too easy to thin or top the shot. So, take more sand than usual. Enter the sand, say, two inches behind the ball rather than an inch and a half— even farther behind on a very severe slope.

**Ball above feet.** This stance forces you to swing flatter, as I said earlier. However, because the sand wedge has so much loft, rather than drawing the ball, you'll pull it left unless you allow for this by aiming right of target. Choke well down on the club so that you don't have to swing on quite as flat a plane. You must avoid closing the blade on impact. Here, weakening the left hand grip can help.

**Ball below feet.** The most difficult example of this type of lie is where your feet are out of the bunker, and the ball is in. Then, you must hold the sand wedge at the end of the grip, stand as close to the ball as possible, really bend those knees, and make a big effort to maintain your knee level until the ball is on its way. You must stay down on this one; if you don't pay attention to this, it's all too easy to straighten your knees and completely miss the shot. To compensate for the push that comes with such a lie, aim more to the left than usual.

## FAIRWAY BUNKERS

AS you get farther away from the hole, there comes a point where you can no longer get the ball up to the hole with a sand wedge, even if you use the "longer shot" technique I described earlier.

If you're still fairly close to the green, the safest shot to play is a regular sand shot with a stronger club. This is especially true if the lie is anything less than perfect. Take a pitching wedge, 9-iron or 8-iron, for example, and open the blade and stance so that you cut across the ball. Aim to enter the sand about three-quarters of an inch behind the ball. By opening the blade you lower the back of the sole so that it strikes the sand first. Put another way, by opening the blade, you can create some "bounce" even on a flat-soled club, so that the club will skid through the sand.

When you're farther back from the green—a full short iron up to wood distance away—then the first consideration must be your lie. If the ball is in a depression, you must blast the ball out with your sand wedge. If the lie is good, then your main concern is to select a club with enough loft to clear the lip of the bunker. Be conservative here—if you doubt a 5-iron can clear the lip, always take a 6-iron. It's far better to get the ball out short of the green in position to pitch or chip and putt for your par than to stay in the bunker.

If I'm playing an iron from a fairway bunker, I set up normally on the shot except that I'll place slightly more weight on the left foot than usual. This helps me make a more descending blow. I also take a wider stance to minimize body movement and weight shift during the swing. You've got to stay very steady over the ball. To compensate for less leg action in the swing, I'll go to one stronger club than normal. In the swing, I try to catch the ball as cleanly as possible. In fact, to make certain I don't hit the ball fat, I strive for the feel of hitting the ball thin, almost topping it.

If I need a lot of distance, then I will take a wood. I position the ball more forward in the stance than normal and concentrate on a square club-to-ball contact.

I fully realize that the techniques I've just outlined for fairway bunkers may be too demanding for many seniors, especially high-handicappers. If you feel the need for some "super safe" techniques from fairway bunkers, then here they are.

*From a fairway bunker, I set up normally except I put a little more weight on the left foot. I take a slightly wider stance so I can stay steady over the ball. I try to catch the ball as cleanly as possible.*

With an iron, set up with a square blade, but play the ball well back in the stance, just a little ahead of the right heel. However, position your hands in the normal position off the inside of the left leg. You're thus "hooding" or taking loft off the club, probably as much as two clubs worth. So, if the shot calls for a 5-iron, hood a 7-iron. Keep slightly more weight on the left foot than the right. Now, go ahead and swing. You'll find that with this setup, it's practically impossible to hit the ball fat, the mistake you want to avoid on these shots. However, as an additional safety measure, keep your eyes on a spot an inch or so in front of the ball, and, on the downswing, key on pulling the left hand through the ball.

With a fairway wood, open the face wide—three-quarters of an inch or so—before taking your normal grip. Play the ball up off your left heel. Aim left of your target and align your feet and shoulders left as well. Now swing back and through along your shoulder line, aiming to strike the sand just behind the

The safest way to play an iron from a fairway bunker is to position the ball well back, the weight favoring the left foot. Look at a spot in front of the bal.

A safe way to play a wood from a fairway bunker is to open the face wide, aim wel left of target, and strike the sand behind the ball. The wood will skid through just like a sand wedge.

PLAY BALL BACK

ball. Opening the face, as I said earlier, creates "bounce" so that the back of the sole will hit the sand before the leading edge. The club will "skid" through the sand just like a sand wedge. You'll get a high slice with this technique, but you'll like the way it clears the lip and the amount of distance you can get out of it.

These two shots may not be elegant, but they work!

## PRESERVE A GOOD WEDGE

I'M not a person big on regrets. However, if I have one it would be that, back in 1961, I had probably the best sand iron of my life. I made the mistake of practicing with that club all the time, and wore it out. What I should have done, I now realize, was to have obtained another one identical to it, and used one for practice, the other for tournament play.

If you do a lot of practicing, I recommend the same idea to you. If you find the sand wedge that works for you, then go out immediately and buy another one that is exactly the same. Come on now, at your age you can afford it!

Believe me, once you try to weld on another flange, the club never comes out the same.

*CHAPTER TEN*

# TURN THREE SHOTS INTO TWO

THERE'S NO DOUBT ABOUT IT. If there's one part of the game where the senior must learn to shine, it's the short game. If I and a sixteen handicapper went out and played as a team—with him hitting the ball within ninety yards of the hole, and with me hitting all the shots from there on in—his handicap would drop to about a seven! For fun, I've played a few holes this way with amateur friends back home, and, if anything, that seven handicap is a little on the *generous* side!

I consider myself fortunate that the importance of having a fine short game was impressed on me at an early age. When I was sixteen, I was playing in the club championship at my club in Johannesburg. My opponent was Alf Green, who must have been about sixty years of age at that time. Alf had lost some length over the years—I outdrove him by some fifty or sixty yards every time. However, he never let it bother him. He kept plonking the ball down the middle, getting it up around the green, and beat me 2 and 1 with such deadly pitching, chipping, and putting that I have never forgotten it.

That's a marvellous lesson for seniors. It doesn't matter if you've lost some length. You can more than make up for it provided you have a finely honed short game.

That was also a marvellous lesson for me, and it immediately put a blueprint for action into my mind. They say, "You drive for show, and putt for dough," but this experience made me realize that *everything's* for dough, and *especially* short game shots. I began spending much more time practicing my wedges, chipping, sand shots, and putting.

The experience also hit home to me because, being small, I

was not a long hitter by professional standards. I began to realize that, even if I wasn't long, I could still compete if my short game was good enough.

This has always been true, of course, but everyone has to learn this lesson for himself. In the 1930s, Sam Snead and Craig Wood were two of the longest hitters the game has ever seen. Yet diminutive Paul Runyan, whom they often outdrove by as much as eighty yards, beat them both in two PGA Championship finals.

In 1934, Runyan beat Wood by 1 up in extra holes. In 1939 he handed Snead the worst beating in the history of the championship, 8 and 7.

Runyan did it with what Snead described to me as, "the most phenomenal work around the greens I've ever seen." Snead told me how he'd have a hole won and then Runyan would sink a chip shot, lay the ball dead from behind a bush, or hole a sixty-foot putt. Snead added that the defeat made him realize that, though long hitting was nice, he'd better get to work on his short game!

Whether you're a long hitter or not, a good striker of the ball or not, a good short game can bail you out when your long game deserts you. You can mishit a lot of wood shots, mishit a lot of irons, but if you can "turn three shots into two," as the British call it, near the green, you'll stay in the ball game.

What brought this to mind was my victory in the 1987 U.S. Senior Open Championship at Brooklawn CC, Fairfield, CT. During the last round, I was playing excellent golf—I was down the middle of the fairway practically all the time, hitting the greens in regulation, and leaving myself the right putts— uphill putts, not tricky downhillers. In contrast, my playing companion and rival for the championship, Chi Chi Rodriguez, was not having a good day. Normally a great driver of the ball, he was in trouble many times off the tee. He missed several greens, but each time, it seemed, he'd pull off a great little pitch or chip and make par. If I hadn't been able to capitalize on my good approach shots by holing the necessary birdie putts to keep my edge on him, the result might have been a lot

**Seniors: The most common failing I see among seniors in the short game is leaving pitch shots short. Aim for the top of the flagstick, not the bottom, and you'll get the ball up to the hole.**

closer. Even so, Chi Chi's marvellous short game kept him in the hunt until he ran out of holes.

The short game starts at the point where you're making something less than a full swing. Basically, we'll cover two types of shots—pitches and chips. A pitch shot, used from the longer distances and to go over traps and other difficulties, is mostly carry and very little run. A chip, used from close to the green, usually has little carry, and a lot of run; you just land the ball on the green, then let it run to the hole.

# PITCHES

ALTHOUGH the pitch shot swing is much like a miniature of the full swing for short irons, there are some differences. As a rule, you're playing the shot with either a pitching wedge or sand wedge. The closer you get to the green, the more you narrow the stance, and make the swing more with the hands and arms and less with the body. Also, the shorter the shot, the more you should choke down on the club for control. To stop the ball, you want to keep more weight on the left foot. This sets you up for a quicker wrist break and a more upright swing, which produces greater height. You also should open the stance so that you hit the ball slightly from out to in, that is, with some cut, or slice spin. Slice spin also helps the ball settle down quickly on the green.

On a normal fairway lie, set the blade square and position the ball about four inches inside the left heel. The hands should be ahead of the ball, programming a downward hit. Set the right knee inward, and hold it there during the swing. Essentially, you swing the arms and hands back around a firm right leg. Then hit down on the ball firmly.

The amount of swing you take depends on your distance from the hole. On a longer pitch, you'd swing your hands back to just above shoulder height, (see illustrations), which is called a three-quarter swing. On shorter pitches, you'd swing your hands back to about waist height or just past your right leg, for what are called half- and quarter-swings.

Like any swing, it's fatal to decelerate into the ball. Therefore, make a point of swinging through at least as far you swing back. If you swing the hands back to shoulder height, swing them through to shoulder height, if you swing them back to

*In pitching, it's essential to make a good, accelerating swing. To do this, you should always swing through at least as far as you swing back.*

waist height, swing them through to waist height, and so on. If anything, err on the side of making the follow-through a little fuller than the backswing. Then you'll know you've accelerated through the ball.

The most common failing among seniors on these shots is to leave them short of the hole. This is either because they made a decelerating swing, just dealt with, or because they aim for the bottom of the flagstick. Instead, any time you're twenty-five yards or farther from the hole, get into the habit of aiming for the *top* of the flag. You'll find this little trick will get you up to the hole just about every time.

The principles I've outlined apply whether you are using a pitching wedge or a sand wedge. However, I must remind you here of what I said earlier in Chapter Five. If you're using a sand wedge with a medium width of sole and a fair amount of bounce, then you shouldn't use it off a bare, hard lie, still less if you want to open the blade. Use a pitching wedge instead, or a third wedge with a flat sole.

With that in mind, let's explore some variations of the basic pitch to meet special situations.

If you need a higher shot than usual, and assuming you have a good lie, play the ball more forward, up off your left heel, open the clubface and open the stance. Have your weight merely favor the left foot, break your wrists sharply off the ball, and hit down firmly on the ball from out to in. Essentially, you play the shot in the same way as a normal greenside bunker shot except that you catch the ball first, then take some turf.

If you're in rough close to the green, and have to carry some rough or bunker in between you and the green, then use the same shot. If you can't hit cleanly on the back of the ball, then play the shot in exactly the same way as a bunker shot, planning to enter the grass behind the ball. What you're doing is using the grass, rather than sand, to cushion the blow. It's worth adding that you can also deliberately hit behind the ball from a poor fairway lie, provided the ground is soft enough to cut through. In both cases, remember that, through impact, the club will encounter more resistance than usual from the grass or ground. Therefore, you'll have to use a longer swing to generate enough force—a rough guide would be to imagine that the ball actually does lie in a bunker.

*To make an extra high pitch, play the ball forward, and open the blade and stance.*

*On most pitches, you want the ball to check. To do that, you must keep the blade open.*

If you need an extra high pitch shot, and assuming a very good lie, play the shot the same way as the higher shot except that this time you keep more weight on the right foot. Instead of the hands being ahead of the ball as on a normal pitch, the hands will be in line with the ball. On the downswing, use the "early flip" action described in Chapter Nine.

If you have a poor lie, then play the ball back in your stance nearer the right foot with your hands well ahead of the ball. This enables you to hit down more. However, it will also result in a lower shot with more run, because you've hooded the blade. If you need a low pitch—say into a stiff wind—then

*If you want a wedge shot to run, let the left hand roll to the left, closing the blade.*

keep the blade square. The wind will stop the ball for you when it lands on the green. If you need more height and stop on the shot, then open the blade and take a more open stance.

Most of the time, you want to stop the ball fairly quickly after it hits the green. You're cutting the ball, either a little or a lot. The last thing you want to do on this kind of shot is for the blade to close through impact. A very important point, therefore, on these shots is to keep the back of the left hand pulling through toward the hole so as to keep the blade open. If you were to let the left hand roll to the left through impact, the blade would close and the ball would run once it landed on the green.

Occasionally, you'll want a wedge shot that rolls more than usual. In that case, open the blade going back, but let the left hand roll to the left coming through. The blade is then closing through impact, and you'll get the run you want. The shot is played like a draw in miniature—a little "open to closed" swing.

## CHIP SHOT STRATEGY

ON chip shots from around the green, I might use any club from a 4-iron to a sand wedge. The exact choice of club will depend on such factors as the ball's lie, the length of the shot, the ground between the ball and green, the amount of green between the ball and hole, and whether the green itself is hard or soft.

Whenever you can, you should plan to land the ball on the green. It's always the best groomed ground on any course, so why take a chance on getting a bad bounce by landing the ball in the fringe?

From my observations, too many seniors play a lofted chip as a matter of habit. Instead, if you have a choice, always favor

**Seniors: On a chip shot, never use a wedge when you can use a lower lofted club. I see this mistake all the time in senior pro-ams. Remember: The less the loft on a club, the less the chance of a mishit, and the better the result if you do mishit.**

a runup over a more lofted shot. Only play a lofted chip if you're forced to—when you're farther away from the green and have little green to work with. There is much less chance of mishitting a less lofted club like a 4-iron than a well lofted club like a wedge. If you do mishit a less lofted iron, generally you still get a pretty good result. Mishit a wedge, however, and you probably "dump" the ball halfway to the hole.

One of the more common mistakes in club selection I see among seniors is when they're, say, fifteen feet off the green and the pin is at the back of the green. Normally, if you're this far off the green, you won't have much green to work with, and will have to use a more lofted club. However, if you have thirty, forty, or fifty feet of green to work with, you can and should use a less lofted club, and run the ball.

As a rule of thumb, always select the club with the least amount of loft that will carry your ball at least a yard onto the green—to give yourself a margin for error—and still not let it roll past the hole.

Although I've said you should always land the ball on the green if you can, there is one major exception to it. If the ground in front of the green is firm and you can rely on getting a dependable bounce, then run the ball with a low lofted club even if you're farther back from the green. This is especially true at British seaside courses in summer. I can't tell you the number of times I've used that shot over there—it's often the percentage shot even if there is no wind. The same can be true in the U.S., especially on harder courses such as you find in Texas. So, always keep your eyes open to the possibility of running the ball, even in America.

While you choose your club, also select the spot on which you want the ball to land. This could be a light or dark patch of turf, anything that gives you a target on which to focus. To select the spot, you must read the green just as you would on a putt, taking into account the speed of the green and any slopes

**Seniors: On chips, the secret of success is to have a clear picture of the whole shot in your mind before you play it. Pick out the spot on which you want the ball to land, "see" yourself making the stroke, then see the ball flying to that spot and rolling into the hole. You'll consistently put the ball so close, it will amaze you.**

or grain. If the green slopes to the left, for example, you must try to land your ball a little to the right of the direct line to the hole.

The next step is to take several practice swings. I've said earlier that seniors should take a couple of practice swings before every shot. This is particularly important on chip shots because every one of these shots is different from another. The best way to prepare for it is by taking practice swings while visualizing the ball flying through the air, landing on the spot, and then rolling into the hole. With each practice swing, you'll find yourself refining, perfecting the stroke. Once you have a clear picture in your mind of the right stroke, then go ahead and hit the ball the same way.

## WRISTY CHIPS

I personally like to use a wristy method of chipping (see photos on page 148).

My setup is very similar to that for the pitch. The stance is fairly narrow, and a trifle open. Again, I choke well down on the club. However, unlike the pitch, where I'm usually cutting the ball, I don't want my shoulders open. Rather, an imaginary line drawn from shoulder to shoulder would be square to the target line so that I can hit straight down the line and put the proper roll on the ball. To help me hit down firmly, the ball is back in my stance, my weight kept on the left foot—I like to feel as though my left foot is nailed to the ground—and my hands are well ahead of the ball, about opposite the crease in my left pants leg. I set my right knee inward to the left, and keep it there during the backswing.

I feel as though I hit the chip with my hands. Going back, I break the wrists, with just enough arm and shoulder to keep the action fluid. On the downswing, I hit down firmly on the ball. You'll note I have very little follow-through, the club finishing low and on line to the hole. This is because, instead of "swinging" the club through, I give the ball a firm "rap."

I use the same "rapping" technique in putting. This is basically because I grew up on very rough Bermuda grass. From such grass, you have to hit wristy chips and putts. By

In the wristy chipping method, use a narrow, open stance, the weight on the left foot. Going back, break the wrists, then hit down firmly, giving the ball a firm "rap."

standardizing my technique in this way, using one type of stroke for both chipping and putting, I simplify my whole short game. The Japanese do the same, because they play on Korai grass, which also has a very rough texture.

## STIFF-WRISTED CHIPS

TODAY, with bent-grass greens predominating, the general improvement in course conditioning, and particularly the manicuring of fringes and greens, most of the golfers on tour use another method of chipping. It's a stiff-wristed action where, instead of hitting down very firmly, the ball is "swept" away (see photos).

When using this method, set up with the weight fairly evenly divided between the feet, with maybe just a little more weight on the left foot. Again, the ball is back in the stance, and the hands slightly ahead of the ball. The key to the swing is that the only moving parts are the arms and shoulders, which take the club back and through. There's no wrist action.

*In the stiff-wristed method, divide the weight evenly between the feet. Only use the arms and shoulders— no wrist action. Make the finish as long as the backswing.*

To ensure an accelerating hit, work on making the follow-through at least as long as the backswing, if anything, a trifle longer.

The golfers who use the stiff-wristed chip will also use a similar method in putting. This makes sense, because it's obviously easier to develop touch around the green if you use one method than if you try to use two. That's why I suggest that, whichever method you elect to use, use it for putts as well as chips.

However, if you choose to go with the wristless method, then only use it if you have a good lie. If you try it when, for example, the ball lies in a small depression, you're likely to half-top the ball. When the ball is lying badly, there is only one way to chip successfully, and that's the wristy method—put your weight on the left foot, hands well ahead, and break your wrists on the backswing. You can then chop the ball out of the bad lie very easily. It's worth noting that, from a poor lie, you usually can't be certain of avoiding all the grass behind the ball. So, plan to land the ball on the green a slightly shorter distance than normal to allow for a slight "flyer" effect and more run than usual.

While I would never say that one of these chipping methods is better than the other, I have been very successful with the wristy, "rapping" method. It has the advantage that it can be used anywhere in the world, on any grasses, rough as well as smooth, and from poor as well as good lies. However, the choice is up to you. If you grew up on bent greens and a finely manicured course, it's likely that you'll have developed a wristless method of putting. In that case, you'll probably find it easier to chip the same way.

## THE TEXAS WEDGE

ONE shot that the senior should really work on is what has become know as the Texas wedge, that is, using the putter from off the putting green. The reason why putting off the fringe is so often the best percentage shot is an extension of the club selection strategy I was talking about earlier. If it's easier to strike a ball more solidly when chipping with a 4-iron than a wedge, then it's easier to strike the ball more solidly with a putter than even a 4-iron. As I've often heard Arnold Palmer say, "Most times, your worst putt is as good as your best chip."

However, you must realize that the Texas wedge is not a panacea for all chipping ills. Use it when the fringe is short and smooth, and the ball is sitting up high in the grass. Use it when the grain of the grass is with you, that is, growing in the direction of the stroke. Certainly, use it from a bare lie, where it's so easy to stub a chip. However, as a general rule, it's advisable to putt the ball only when your ball is within two feet of the edge of the green. The farther away you are from the green, the more difficult it becomes to judge how much harder to hit the ball to roll it through the fringe.

You should avoid using the putter if the ball is lying down in the grass or the grain is against you. Then, use my wristy chip. When you have these types of lies, don't ground your club. Instead, hover the club behind the ball. Then you can easily hit down on it.

## CHIPPING FAULTS

IN chipping, the worst fault I see among seniors is "cupping" the left wrist coming through the ball. In other words, the left wrist breaks down and there's a big, concave curve in the wrist. Usually, this comes from an effort to "scoop" the ball up with the right hand. You'll soon know if you're doing this as you'll usually hit your chips "fat," and sometimes thin or even top them. "Scooping" can occur whichever chipping method you use. If you haven't played for a while, then you must guard against this fault. You are most likely to "scoop" when you're a little out of practice and have lost some of your normal confidence.

If this is your problem, then keep your eyes on the front of the ball—this will encourage you to hit down on the ball. Also, in practice try this: Choke down on the club, put the butt of the club against the inside of your left forearm and keep it

---

**Seniors: One of the best ways to improve your short game is to compete against a friend and have a little bet going. I do this all the time when I'm at home. You should, too. It's great for your short game and a marvellous way to fill a summer evening.**

*A great tip is to practice chipping from a bunker. If you don't keep your head still and catch the ball first, the ball will go nowhere!*

there during the swing. Hit several chips this way. You'll soon get the feeling of keeping your left wrist firm through the ball. If "scooping" strikes you out on the course, a few practice swings done this way will quickly put you straight.

Mishitting chips can also be caused by moving the head and body, another common fault among seniors. Remember: The closer you get to the green, the steadier you must keep the head, and the less you must move the body.

If you're always moving around too much when chipping, you might try turning both feet inward into a pigeon-toed stance. This will help you eliminate the excess body movement.

Finally, another very good cure is our old friend, practicing from a bunker. I do this all the time and can't recommend it to you too highly. If you don't keep your head still and down, if you don't catch the ball first, it will go nowhere!

## MAKE PRACTICE FUN

I'M a great believer in having fun while practicing. You concentrate best when you're enjoying yourself.

Whenever I'm home in South Africa, I often have a match, as I've said, with my friend Fardel Allem. However, after our rounds is when the best fun begins. We go back to his ranch, where he has a practice green, and we play against each other in chipping, putting, and bunker play. Of course, I give him a handicap.

Our bet in these matches is a little unusual; at dinner that evening, the loser has to wait on the winner! If he beats me, for example, I must pull out his chair for him and seat him. If he says, "Waiter, I need a glass of water," I have to get up and fetch it, and so on. Neither of us relishes being the waiter, so we play our hearts out in these games! It really keeps my short game sharp.

## CHAPTER ELEVEN

# *INTO THE HOLE*

P UTTING IS THE ONE PART OF THE GAME where every senior should break par. I don't care whether you're scratch or thirty-six handicap, whether you're forty, sixty, or even eighty years old. Even though par allows you thirty-six putts per round, two on every green, don't be lulled into thinking that thirty-six putts is good putting. It isn't. The statistics leaders on the PGA Tour average about twenty-nine putts a round when hitting 12–13 greens in regulation (to hit a green in regulation, you must reach a par 3 hole in one stroke, a par 4 in two strokes, and a par 5 in three strokes). Since you probably don't hit as many greens in regulation as a pro, good putting for you is certainly no more than twenty-nine putts.

To achieve this goal, you need to work on three main objectives—a good stroke, a careful reading of the green, and a good mental attitude. All three are just as important as any of the others. You could have the finest, most repetitive stroke in the world, but if you're careless with your "read," or feel you're a poor putter, you won't make much headway.

## A GOOD STROKE

AS with the golf swing, defining a good stroke at first seems extremely difficult, if not impossible. Probably the finest putters I ever saw were Bobby Locke and Arnold Palmer. However, Locke stood up to the ball with a very closed stance, took the club back to the inside, with a fairly long backswing, and gave the impression of "hooking" his putts. He would "die" the ball into the hole; it would almost creep up to the cup and fall in on what seemed like its last turn. On the other hand, when Arnold was in his prime, he stood up to the ball with a square, knock-kneed stance, and used a wristy, very aggressive stroke. He banged most putts so hard that, if they missed, they would finish up to six feet past the hole. He seldom missed the "comeback" putts. Arnold invented TV's "seventy-foot birdie putt," because he seemed to be able to make any putt when he needed it.

I could go on, and describe the long, flowing arm and shoulder action of Ben Crenshaw, the wristy, jabbing action of Billy Casper, the aggressive stiff-wristed stroke of Tom Watson, the deliberate stroke of Jack Nicklaus, but the point is that the great putters appear to use such different methods that it would appear that there cannot be any hard and fast rules.

That's how I felt myself as a young man. Today, with over thirty years of observing the great putters, I can identify seven major qualities that the great putters' strokes have in common. They give one a good starting point.

## WHAT THE GREAT PUTTERS DO

**1. An unvarying routine.** I've talked about "routine" in regard to the shots up to the green. However, in putting, you should also develop your own step-by-step method of taking your stance and stroking the ball. I remember Locke particularly in this regard. On every putt, whether it was in a friendly match or the last stroke in a championship, he'd take his two practice swings, then step up to the ball and hit it without delay. His routine never varied, and neither should yours. By sticking to your routine, you keep your mind on the task at hand—visualizing how to stroke this putt so it goes into the hole—and avoid any negative thoughts. It also helps you set up the same way every time, which makes for a more consistent stroke.

**2. Thumbs on top.** Many great putters use the reverse overlap grip, as I do myself. I like it because, with the left forefinger lapping over the fingers of my right hand, my whole grip feels unified. However, Locke, for one, used the regular overlap, so the type of grip is not an absolute. The one thing that is common to all great putters is that they put the thumbs on the top of the grip, not on the sides. This is because the thumbs of each hand are the "feelers." When you feel the texture of cloth, or when reaching into your pocket for a particular type of coin, it's your thumb that does the feeling. When the thumbs are on top of the grip, you get the best feel out of them. Many great putters also position the thumbs straight down the shaft—this ensures that both palms are parallel to each other so that the hands work together.

**3. Eyes over the ball.** Most great putters either keep their eyes over the ball, or at least over the target line. This makes sense because then you get a true picture of the line and you're far more likely to aim correctly. Also, if you stand too far away, so that the eyes are inside the target line, you're likely to fan the putter open on the backswing and roll it closed on the downswing, making square contact more difficult. Conversely, if you stand too close, you're likely to swing from shut to open. If your eyes are over the ball, you have a far better chance of keeping the club squarer during the stroke. A very good way to test where your eyes are positioned is to take your address, then, without moving your feet or head, take hold of the putter with your index finger and thumb and suspend the putter from the bridge of your nose.

**4. Head still, body still.** I have only seen one great putter who moved his body during the stroke, and that was Locke. However, I truly believe he was the exception that proves the rule. All the others had no trace of sway in their action. This is because what's needed in putting is a precise hit—you don't need a great deal of power. Excess body movement merely complicates your task. A good feeling to have is that your legs are set in cement. If you find it difficult to keep your body quiet, then try Palmer's knock-kneed stance. Alternatively, try putting most of your weight on one foot or the other. For example, I set up in a narrow, very closed stance with my weight on my left heel, whereas Chi Chi Rodriguez has recently changed to a narrow, very open stance, also with more weight on the left foot. Chi Chi's new stance, interestingly, is much like that of great putters back at the turn of the century and earlier.

As an aside, Chi Chi developed this stance, he says,

*With his new putting style, Chi Chi Rodriguez has won ten Senior Tour events in two years.*

from watching Jack Nicklaus putt. Like Nicklaus, Chi Chi is right eye dominant. With a conventional square stance, Chi Chi had to turn his head to the left to see the line to the hole—his nose blocked his sight of it out of his dominant eye. Now, with the open stance, he can set up slightly behind the ball, as Jack does, with his head turned slightly to the left. He can see the whole line clearly without any head movement.

The change has done wonders for Chi Chi's putting. Earlier, I told you of his marvellous chips and pitches in the stretch at the 1987 U.S. Senior Open. His putting was just as good. Because his approach shots from the rough often left him putts from above the hole, awkward, fast downhillers, he at times stroked the ball four, even six feet past the hole, but he holed so many of these "knee-knockers" coming back, it was incredible.

Another moral to this story is that you're never too old to learn. As Chi Chi told me, "Putting was always my downfall on the PGA Tour. If I could have putted well, I might have won 50 tournaments and at least one major, instead of just eight." On the Senior PGA Tour, Chi Chi has already won ten tournaments with his new putting style and confidence in just his second full year on the tour, including two majors, the 1986 Seniors Tournament Players Championship and the 1987 PGA Seniors Championship!

**5. Never go back outside.** I've never known a great putter take the putter back outside the intended line of putt. This causes you either to cut across the ball, and you get a lot of skid and sidespin on the putt, or you pull the ball to the left with a closed clubface. To putt consistently, you must either take the putter straight back or slightly inside the line. However, it's worth adding that many golfers who think they're taking the putter straight back and through, are actually taking it back outside! So, taking the putter back slightly inside is a lot safer.

**6. Accelerate through.** I said earlier that, in the full swing, a tentative effort will never give a good result. The same applies in putting. I've never seen a great putter who consistently made a "powder-puff" swing, or "dropped" the putter head on the ball. However, I've seen many, many poor putters who do just that, and, as a result, never put a good roll on the ball and invariably leave the ball short. You must accelerate through the ball.

**7. A repeating stroke.** A great putter's stroke repeats, repeats and repeats. This is something you must train yourself to do when practicing. You cannot get good results if you take a long pendulum-like swing one time and a shorter, more aggressive swing another. You can't hit one putt on the sweet spot and the next off the toe. So much of putting is to develop a good feel for distance. You can only do this if you groove a repeating stroke.

As in chipping, you basically have two choices in the type of putting stroke you use—a wristy style or the wristless arm and shoulder style.

## WRISTY STYLE

AS I've said, I personally use the wristy style of putting, and "rap" the ball firmly. I've used it all my life with the exception of one brief period in 1978. With the wristless style, I won the Masters that year, and then the next two tournaments on the PGA Tour, the Tournament of Champions and Houston Open. However, not long afterward, I decided it was not for me and returned to the wristy method. One particular reason I prefer "rap" putting for seniors is that a stiff-wristed, long smooth stroke is difficult for people over fifty, as their nerves are generally not good enough.

I personally set up with a closed stance. This is because I never want to cut a putt. The closed stance helps me, even reminds me, to take the putter back to the inside, but, I should add, it doesn't *make* me take the club back inside. Your hands can take the putter back outside whatever your stance. The closed stance helps, but you have to *learn* to take it back inside.

That's why, though I recommend a closed stance to everyone, I'm not going to be too dogmatic about it. In fact, I know that many golfers find it easier to set up with their shoulders square to the line if they use a square stance. In the accompanying photos, I posed with more of a square stance because I felt that most golfers would more readily identify with them.

Normally, I position the ball off my left foot. However, on breaking putts, you should protect against missing the hole on the low side. On a putt that breaks from right to left, either because of a slope or grain, I position the ball a little bit back in my stance. This keeps my hands ahead of the ball and prevents me from pulling the ball to the left. On putts that will break

from left to right, I play the ball a little forward to guard against pushing the ball to the right.

On the backswing, I hood the club a little, that is, there is a little counterclockwise turning of the wrists along with the wrist break. I've found that, if you hood the club, you'll get the ball up to the hole ten times easier than if you didn't. The turning action that causes the hooding enables you to release on the putt, and you roll the ball far better. I should add that many other great putters have hooded the blade, including Walter Hagen, Bobby Locke, Billy Casper, and Arnold Palmer.

When I come back to the ball, I believe you should just rap it, and not have much, if any, follow-through. (For the record, Locke, Casper and other fine putters such as Doug Ford and Bob Rosburg also rapped their putts.)

I clearly remember watching Casper on the putting green before we played in the 1962 PGA Championship at Aronomink GC, Newtown Square, PA. As I've told you, I had always tended to "rap" my putts. However, in watching Billy, I noticed that, if anything, he was just a little firmer than I was in "rapping" the ball. I decided then and there to make my putting style more closely conform to his. It paid rich dividends. I was fortunate enough to win that PGA with a score of 278, my third major.

*In the wristy style of putting, stroke the ball with your hands and wrists giving it a firm "rap."*

Having taken the club to the inside, I come into the ball from the inside. As I hit the ball, I almost get the feeling that I'm putting hook spin on it. In other words, if anything, the stroke is a little in to out. As a matter of scientific fact, it is impossible to hook a ball on the green, to actually make it roll with a curve from right to left. However, I'm certain that, if you *feel* that you're hooking your putts a little, you'll put the best roll on the ball. Seve Ballesteros, among other great putters I've talked to, says he gets the same "hook" feel.

## WRISTLESS STYLE

IF you use the wristless method of putting, then plant the feet about two feet apart, as I'm doing in the photos. The stance should be square, or very slightly open. In the stroke, you swing the putter as though it were an extension of the left arm. Again, the only moving parts are the arms and shoulders. The swing is much like the swing of a pendulum. The backswing and follow-through should at least be of the same length, or, if anything, the follow-through should be a trifle longer.

*In the wristless style, you stroke the ball with arm and shoulder action only. Keep the wrists firm.*

It's interesting to note that some of the best wristless putters also hood the club on the backswing. For example, former British Open Champion Bob Charles, still one of the finest putters you'll ever see, hoods the blade. Also, on long putts, most wristless putters will use a little wrist. Ben Crenshaw, for one, has told me he does this. First, it's difficult to get enough feel on longer putts without any wrist action, and second, most golfers find they can't develop enough force to get the ball up to the hole without some wrist to supplement the arm and shoulder action.

In the same way, a wristy putter couldn't get the ball up to

**Seniors: If you grew up playing on bent greens, you probably developed a wristless stroke. If you then retire (or relocate) to an area with Bermuda greens and find you can't putt on them, try my wristy, "rapping" method. Take it from someone who grew up on grainy greens!**

the hole on a very long putt if he just used wrist action. He has to supplement the wrists with some arm and shoulder action.

While I won't push one type of stroke on you at the expense of the other, you may wonder why I chose to go back to the wristy style later in 1978. Well, it was not just that I was reluctant to abandon a method that works equally well on any type of green—whether Bermuda grass or bent grass in the U.S., the very true greens at the British seaside, the very grainy greens in South Africa and Japan—although that is part of the answer. What it came down to was this: For me, at least, the wristless style, with its longer backswing and follow-through, could easily deteriorate into too sloppy a stroke, one where I decelerated into the ball. When I'm under the gun, and need a five-footer to win a championship, that style could leave me short of the hole. With the wristy style, the whole action is more compact, and there's less possibility of deceleration—or other error— creeping in.

## COMMON STROKE ERRORS

AS in chipping, the most common error seniors make in putting is "cupping" the left wrist at impact. This fault can occur whether you use the wristy or wristless method. If you have this problem, you'll probably be either "thinning" or pulling your putts left. A quick fix for this is to grip a little firmer with the left hand. However, if that doesn't work, then try a cross-handed grip, with the left hand below the right, as used by Bruce Lietzke. This encourages the left hand to pull through the ball, and keeps the left wrist firm. You could also try Johnny Miller's method, which involves an extra long putter, which is locked in place under the left armpit and against the inside of the left arm.

If you consistently hit the ball to the right or left of the hole, address a straight, shortish putt, say, about seven or eight feet, and then have a friend hold the club in position so you can go behind the ball and check your aim—whether the blade is squarely aligned to the hole or not. Many seniors, I've found, misaim the putter. Also, have your friend check your shoulder alignment. If your shoulders are open, for example, you'll generally swing the club from out to in, and cut or pull the ball.

## THE "YIPS"

THE "yips" is a diabolical complaint afflicting the smaller muscles of the right hand and wrist. At best, it's rather like "scooping" a chip and can cause you to miss just about every short putt you look at. At worst, I've seen golfers yank the ball right off the green with an involuntary twitch of the right hand! Since the "yips" usually strikes golfers past the first flush of youth, we'd better deal with it.

---

**Seniors: If you "yip" your putts, don't despair. Try Sam Snead's "side-saddle" putting style or Charlie Owens' style. In both methods, you putt with the whole right arm, without any wrist action. This effectively removes the "yipping" muscles from the stroke.**

The late Henry Longhurst, the famed English golf writer, once wrote a hilarious article on the subject. In the article, Henry elaborated on the famous golfers who have been afflicted with this dreaded putting disease, including Tommy Armour, Leo Diegel, Sam Snead, Ben Hogan, and the immortal Harry Vardon.

Vardon, the winner of six British Opens and one U.S. Open, described his symptoms thus in his book from 1912, *How to Play Golf.* "As I stood addressing the ball I would watch for my

*Charlie Owens' new putter and putting style are the best solution yet to the "yips."*

right hand to jump. At the end of two seconds I would not be looking at the ball at all. My gaze would have become riveted on my right hand. I simply could not resist the desire to see what it was going to do. Directly, as I felt that it was about to jump, I would snatch at the ball in a desperate effort to play the shot before the involuntary movement could take effect. Up would go my head and body with a start and off would go the ball, anywhere but on the proper line."

Longhurst concluded his article with the words used as the title for the piece, "Once you've had 'em, you've got 'em." In other words, there was no known cure.

Today, thankfully, this conclusion is out of date. In the last few years, new putters and putting styles have overcome the problem. What makes these methods work is that they take the "yipping" muscles—those of the right hand and wrist—completely out of the stroke.

The first true solution to the problem was the "croquet" putter, where you faced the hole, straddled the line, and putted forward between the legs. When straddling the line was banned, Sam Snead introduced a variation of the "croquet" method which he called his "sidesaddle" style. He put his feet together and played the ball slightly forward of and to the right of the right foot. He held the top of the putter with his left hand, the thumb on the butt of the club, then extended his right arm so that his right hand held the putter halfway down the shaft. He then made the stroke with the whole right arm, with no wrist action.

However, I would say that, while Snead's method suits him well, it might be difficult for someone less supple. Also, although his method works well up to ten feet, it's difficult to get the ball up to the hole on longer putts.

Recently, Charlie Owens, one of the stars on the Senior Tour, designed a new, extra long (fifty inches) and heavy (three and a half pounds) putter and a new putting method to go along with it. Many golfers on the Senior Tour formerly afflicted with the yips are now putting well again with his "Slim Jim" putter. You stand to the side of the ball, as in the normal stroke. However, you anchor the top end of the putter with your left hand against your breastbone, the left forearm across the chest. The right arm is extended so that, as in the Snead method, you make the stroke with the whole right arm.

Because you stand tall with Charlie's putter, the method is easy on the back and doesn't require extraordinary flexibility. In my view, it's the best solution to the "yips" I've yet seen.

## READING THE GREEN

READING the green, especially if you're playing a strange course, should start in the pro shop before you go to the first tee. Talk to the local professionals; they know their course best. They may tell you, for example, that the slope of the greens is away from the mountains, toward the sea, or that the grain of the green—the direction in which the grass grows—is with the prevailing wind and so on. They can also tell you if there are any exceptions to such general rules.

As you approach each green, you should note the general slope of the terrain, if any. Later, if you're in any doubt about the break of a putt, go with this general slope.

On the green, start by reading the putt from behind the ball looking toward the hole. Note any slopes and try to form a mental picture of how the ball will run. Will it go straight or break to the left or right?

Refine this picture by walking to a point about midway to the hole and fifteen feet to the side of your line. From here, you can see whether the putt is flat, or if uphill or downhill, how sharp a slope is involved. If you're putting uphill, you have to stroke the ball harder, and allow for less break than on a level putt. On a downhill putt, you must stroke more softly and allow for more break.

Then, you should take a long look in the hole itself. Many of my senior pro-am partners ask me, "Why do you do that?" I think they suspect that this is either a mannerism of mine or perhaps I'm killing time until I've made up my mind on that putt! This is not so. You can learn an enormous amount by looking in the hole, as you'll now see.

First, check the depth of soil above the cup. If there is a deeper layer on one side than the other, you know that, as the ball nears the hole, the putt will break to the side with less soil. This is because course superintendents will always try to set the cup as upright as possible so that the flagstick will also be erect. If the green is not level, there will always be more soil showing above the cup on the high side of the hole than the low side.

Second, take a good look at the grass around the edge of the hole. If there is more wear on one side than the other, then you know that most putts have hit that side. Since the balls will hit the low side of the hole more often and harder than the high side, the side with more wear is the low side.

Looking in the hole can also help you read the grain, the direction in which the grass grows. On Bermuda greens, the grass lies flat instead of growing upright and there's a lot of grain, so it becomes extremely important to be able to read the grain. Against the grain, a putt will roll much slower, down grain or with the grain, much faster, and on cross grain putts the ball will break in the direction of the grain just as if you were putting on a side slope.

As with slope, first look for the side of the hole that has more wear. That side is the downgrain side, since balls will hit the downgrain side of the hole more often and harder than the upgrain side. Second, you should realize that, when the hole is cut, the root system of the grass will be severed on the downgrain side. Therefore, the side of the cup where the grass has died (has gone brown) indicates the downgrain side.

Here are some other ways in which you can read grain. If you look downgrain, the green will have a bright, silvery appearance. If you look up- or against the grain, you'll see patches of dark green grass. You can also test the fringe of the green by brushing your putter back and forth in the grass to determine the grain. In my experience, the direction of grain on the fringe is always the same as that on the green itself. However, don't brush your putter on the green. That's contrary to the Rules of Golf.

Besides slope and grain, you should also take into consideration two other factors, the pace of the green and wind.

As regards pace, train yourself to check the length of the grass and always observe other players' chips and putts to help you assess whether the greens are slow or fast.

On a fast green, you must hit the ball less hard and thus any slopes will affect the putt more. On slow, or wet, greens you should play for less break and hit the ball more firmly.

Wind, too, can affect a putt—the stronger the wind, the more you have to allow for it. It's worth noting that in a big wind, besides allowing for its effect on the ball, you should also take a wider stance than usual for extra stability.

My last word on "reading" a green is: Be decisive. If you read a six-inch left-to-right break on a putt, don't change your mind when you get over the ball. Your first impressions on the line are usually correct. Never second-guess yourself!

A perfect example of what I mean occurred at the 1987 Senior Tournament Players Championship at Sawgrass CC, Jacksonville, FL. We came down to the last hole. Chi Chi Rodriguez was in with his score. My playing partner, Bruce Crampton, then missed his putt, and tied Chi Chi. I was left with an eight-footer straight down the hill for all the marbles. If I had second-guessed myself about it being a straight putt—perhaps imagined a break that wasn't there—I would certainly have missed it. Fortunately, I didn't. I had read the putt as straight, and knocked it right in the back of the hole for the win. It wasn't easy, mind you, with Bruce and Chi Chi watching like hawks and readying themselves for a playoff, but thankfully I managed to pull it off.

# THE MENTAL SIDE

THE most important thing in putting is a positive mental attitude. On every putt, "see" the ball going into the hole in your mind's eye. Paint a picture of the whole line from ball to hole and imagine the ball rolling down that line and dropping in.

To help me see the line more clearly, I find it a big help to putt over a spot. Before I step in and address the ball, I pick out a spot on my chosen line about a foot in front of the ball. Then, when I'm setting up, I find it easier to set up square. I can first square the blade to the line to the spot, then set up with my shoulders square to that line. It's worth noting that many great golfers, including Nicklaus, use this "spot" system of alignment throughout their game.

As a general rule, you should always aim for the ball to finish past the hole. There are several reasons for this. First, and most obviously, a ball that doesn't reach the hole, can't fall in; the "never up, never in" thought. Second, if you're past the hole, you'll have stroked the ball firmer. A firmer stroke is a better stroke. Third, if you miss the hole and the ball does go past, the return putt will have the same break as your first putt. Always study the roll of your putts carefully, especially if it appears the ball is going to miss the hole. Don't do that "turn away and groan" routine, you'll miss the break on the "come-backer"!

On short putts, play for the back edge of the hole. It's the same principle as pitching a penny into a bucket—you'd always aim for the back edge, not the front. You must be firm on these putts; this allows you to play less break. As a general rule, keep the ball "inside" the hole on all putts inside six feet, unless, of course, there's a very big break. If you're playing late in the day, and there's been a lot of traffic, you'll have to putt through a lot of spike marks. Then, unless you have a severe downhill putt on your hands, it usually pays to err on the side of hitting the ball too firmly; in that way you will minimize the effect of the spike marks. "Hit and hark" is another excellent tip on these shorties. One of the commonest errors is to look up, and let the body slide forward. You won't do that if you're waiting to hear the sound of the ball rattling in the hole.

The longer the putt, the more important the correct amount of force you need becomes. Most three-putts come from leaving the ball short or past the hole rather than getting the wrong line. I think this happens because golfers get so concerned with the line, they forget to visualize the right strength. A good practice on longer putts is to separate line and strength into two activities. Once you've determined the correct line, set up to your spot and then concentrate all your attention on the right strength of stroke and stroking the ball solidly.

On some putts, say from the lower level to the back level of a two-tier green, it's difficult to get yourself to hit the ball hard enough. If so, imagine a hole that is beyond the actual hole. You can use the same sort of a mental trick on downhill putts —imagine a hole short of the actual hole. Bobby Locke taught me this.

I've found it useful to adopt a philosophical approach to putting. The green is not a perfect surface like a billiard table. On a good putting green, one scientific study revealed that a putting machine will miss 2 percent of six-foot putts, 50 percent of twenty-footers, and 80 percent of sixty-footers. For professionals, the figures were: 45 percent missed from six feet, 88 percent missed from twenty feet and 97 percent from sixty feet. If you miss a putt of six feet or less, it will nearly always be your fault. However, from longer distances, many putts are going to miss whether you made an error or not.

So, tell yourself that only two things can happen on any putt—you can make or miss. If you hole it, fine. If you miss, try to determine your mistake, especially if it's obvious, and learn from it, but then put it behind you!

You can then approach the next putt in the right way— you'll try to hole it. As I've said, you'll come far closer by doing that than by using any other thought.

When you finish your round, get in the habit of talking about your good putts during the round. You'll then create and reinforce a self-image of being a good putter. This is most important. If you believe you're a good putter, you'll be a good putter.

## PUTTING PRACTICE

TO make your putting practice productive, always make it as interesting as possible. Only practice things that keep your interest level high and make you concentrate.

For example, put one ball down eighteen inches from the hole, another two feet away, and others three, five, seven and ten feet out. Then attempt to hole each ball in succession. If you miss one, start again from eighteen inches.

*On putts of thirty feet or less, aim for a semicircle with a two-foot radius, as shown.*

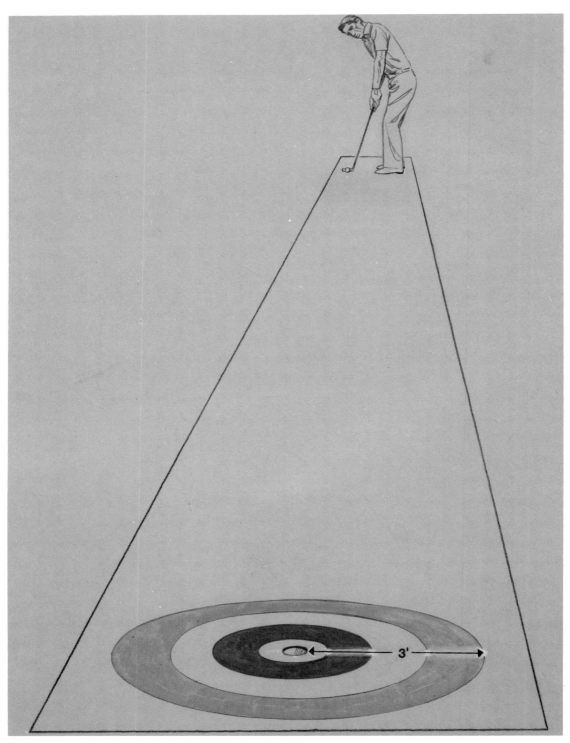

*On putts of more than thirty feet, aim for a circle around the hole with a three-foot radius.*

In a similar vein, set your own personal record for your practice putting course. At first, this might only be thirty-six putts for eighteen holes. However, as you keep on trying to beat your record, your putting will get sharper. Also, there's nothing better than playing matches against your friend on the practice green, and having a little bet going in these matches to provide incentive.

If you're working on a particular length of putt, give yourself a target so that you can measure progress (see illustrations).

If you're practicing putts of thirty feet or less, aim for a semicircle with a two-foot radius and count the number of balls out of ten that you leave in the target area and those that are short or long. On longer putts, aim for a circle with a three-foot radius. Anywhere in this circle is good. Count the number of balls out of ten where you're in the circle. Make a note of these numbers. Then you'll have standards which you can improve.

## ANALYZE YOUR SHORT GAME

ALTHOUGH I've got no quarrel with golfers who like to keep statistics on their whole game—drives in the fairway, greens in regulation, and so on—for most of you seniors, it's more beneficial to keep statistics only on your short game.

On putts, count your total number per round, and how many times you take one putt and more than two putts. On pitches, chips, and bunker shots, count the number of times you get the ball up and down in two strokes, and the number of times you need two putts or more. On all of these shots, also note whether you were short of or past the hole.

Hopefully, these statistics will inspire you to practice your short game more than anything else. I'm not saying this just because the short game is the most productive part of the game to practice. I think it also makes sense, as you get older, to limit the number of full practice shots you hit. You need to conserve your energy. By practicing your short game more, your practice will be less exhausting. You can practice longer with less fatigue.

# MENS SANA IN CORPORE SANO

## CHAPTER TWELVE

# CHOICES—IT'S YOUR LIFE

G OLF IN MANY WAYS is a microcosm of life. No one but you controls your destiny. If you want to get the most out of your golf—and your life—it's important to realize one thing: Every day, when you get up in the morning, you have choices you can make. For example, you can decide to be happy or sad, positive or negative, productive or idle, fit or unfit. I think it's important, first, to recognize that there are such choices; second, of course, to choose wisely.

These choices are important at any age, but they're particularly important for seniors. As we get older, it seems that it's all too easy to become a "moaner." Maybe you can't hit the ball as far as you once could, maybe you can't recover from the rough the way you did when you were younger, but I think the trick is to see your golf—and life—in terms of what you *can* do, not what you can't. Believe me, you can hold onto strength or even build it at any age; you can turn any negative thought into a positive if you work at it. It often does need a conscious effort, but it's well worth it.

Between happy or sad, the obvious choice is happy. However, I fully realize that this is not always as easy as it sounds. We all get down sometimes, or start feeling sorry for ourselves. When this happens to you, here's a marvellous way to "kick" yourself back into a happier frame of mind: *Just think of others in this world who have a tougher life than you do.*

For example, whenever I get down, I look at a photo I have of Bobby Weiland, the man who completed the Boston Marathon—with no legs! He "ran" the distance on his (padded)

> **Seniors: Don't become a grouch on the golf course—your bad shots will bother you too much, and you won't play well. Instead, enjoy your golf, have fun! You'll play far better.**

hands, with a big leather pad for his derriere, and it took him over four days to do it. Out of a field of 19,413, he finished 19,413th. In 1987, he duplicated the feat in the New York Marathon! His example not only makes me realize how blessed I am, it's also a great source of inspiration.

Another antidote I recommend is to think of that old Chinese saying, "All things will pass." That's turned me around quite a few times, I remember, and I'm sure it will do the same for you.

Of course, preventive medicine is even better. I think it's important to associate with people who are happy. Happiness is contagious. When I play practice rounds on the Senior Tour, I play with good players, yes, but more important, I play with people who *enjoy* their golf. I stay away from grouches or anyone who lets the game make them miserable, and so should you.

In fact, come to think about it, I've seen far too many senior amateurs who take the game far too seriously. I don't mean you shouldn't work at your golf, try to improve, and play your heart out on the course. Of course you should. Anything worth doing at all is worth doing to the best of your ability. However, there's no point in letting one bad stroke or even some bad holes upset you to the point where you're no longer fun to play with. After all, you're not playing golf for a living, so don't let a bad round ruin your day—and other people's—or worse, take it home with you. It's over, so put it behind you. Then, you'll be in the right frame of mind to analyze your mistakes so you can do better next time.

For you grouches, here's another reason why you should enjoy your golf. If you let the game become too important to you, then you become so tightly wound, you almost explode after a bad shot. Your mistakes upset you too much and cause you to make further bad shots. However, if you're having fun with your golf—and by this I don't mean that you have to laugh and joke your way round the course, but simply enjoy the challenge of each stroke and the match—you are much more tolerant of your bad shots. You can then get on with the next shot with little fuss—and with a far better chance of success. When you take good and bad in your stride like this, your mind is actually working at its peak level. You concentrate properly and, as a result, you get the most out of your physical game, too. Peter Thomson puts it this way, "Your mind works the best when you're happiest." I couldn't agree more.

A marvellous example of this occurred at the 1987 U.S. Senior Championship. You may remember seeing Chi Chi Rodriguez and I doing a peculiar type of "handshake"; we faced each other, then moved until we were side by side, each bent his right leg backward, and then we "shook hands" with the other's right foot. Incidentally, it was my South African friend Fardel Allem who invented it—that's our "golfer's handshake" on our evening practice sessions. Anyway, I had showed Chi Chi how Fardel and I did it. He was much amused. Then, out on the course, without a word spoken, it suddenly occurred to both of us that this was the right moment to unveil it to the gallery and TV viewers! Here we were, battling it out for a major senior championship, but before we knew it, we were doing it! I shall always treasure that moment—it was fun, and somehow so right. Incidentally, I've also done the "handshake" with Doug Sanders in competition. There's another guy who knows how to have fun while also trying to beat you in the worst possible way!

Similarly, given the choice between being positive or negative, choose positive. For example, I like to have dinner with pros that are good putters, and who talk about how well they putt. I stay away from the guys who tell you how many putts they missed.

It's a funny thing, but where there's a negative there's always a positive—if you really dig for it. For example, recently I was in the locker room after my round and asked a fellow Senior Tour pro, "How did you play today?" He told me he had shot 70, but had missed three three-footers. "I just played the short ones badly," he added. Then I asked him how he had played each hole. It turned out that he actually had holed seven great putts in the course of the round! Yet, all I had been hearing about were the three putts that "got away." With this type of thinking, all he was doing was teaching himself how to be a poor putter. He should have been saying to himself, "I made seven great putts today."

If you tend to be a "moaner," try this "negative to positive" technique. It could change your whole life, as well as your putting!

*Chi Chi Rodriguez and Gary do the "golfer's handshake" at the 1987 U.S. Senior Open.*

The positive approach applies to everything you do. You can fill your mind with good thoughts or abuse it with bad ones. You can put your faith in God or worry needlessly. You can work at your marriage and family life or you can neglect them. You can set high goals and be productive or drift through life never achieving what you might—and should have—done considering your gifts. One of the greatest living examples of the positive approach I've known is my long-time caddie Alfred "Rabbit" Dyer; "Rabbit" has such a pleasant manner, always accentuates the positive and is a great source of confidence to those around him.

I think the key to a happy, productive life is having multiple goals. One of my original goals in life was to win all four Grand Slam tournaments. However, when I achieved that, I didn't start looking for retirement communities. This is because I had other goals that sustained me after the Grand Slam was behind me. They included: being the leading money winner on the U.S. Tour, the most successful golfer on an international basis, winning as many majors as I could, and so on.

You've got to have more than one goal in life. Otherwise, you'll be crushed if you never achieve your goal, or simply spin your wheels if you do achieve it.

Setting your goals high is also important. I once heard of Johnny Miller telling a story about me that is both amusing and instructive. "Gary would have you believe that he exercises eight hours a day, practices ten hours a day, and so on. If he's playing golf as well, there aren't enough hours in the day to do it all!" However, Johnny did go on to say that there was a lot of method to my "madness." By setting almost impossible standards for myself, I made certain that every minute of the day was productive. That's exactly the point. The higher your goals, the more you'll achieve, even if you don't realize your every goal.

You also need goals beyond your current goals. Continuously set goals. That's one of the big secrets of keeping young.

For example, as I neared my fiftieth birthday, I started setting goals as a senior player. These included being the first to win a regular major as a senior as well as making a senior Grand Slam. Well, I'm still working on that first one! However, I've made some headway on the second, having won the PGA Seniors Championship in 1986, and the Senior Tournament Players Championship and the USGA Senior Open in 1987. Now, I want that British Senior Open! Although there is no "official" senior Grand Slam, and probably won't be for some years, I'm willing to bet that these four championships will be the ones recognized in the future.

Another of my goals is related to fitness. I want to get to sixty years of age and have the young guys on the PGA Tour say of me, "Isn't Player incredible! I hope I'm as fit and play as well when I get to sixty!" That's a goal I really want, and the beauty of it is that it will keep me going for a long while yet. When I near sixty, I'll change that goal to seventy, and so on! I'll continue as long as God gives me the strength.

One of the people who inspired me to set such a goal was, of course, Sam Snead, who despite some physical problems, still loves to play, and play well. As the Scottish say, "*Lang may his lum reek!*" (Long may his chimney smoke!)

At the start of this second section, I quoted a famous saying from Juvenal, a Roman poet: "*Mens sana in corpore sano,*" meaning "A sound mind in a sound body." It has always appealed to me because it expresses a fundamental truth: With a sound body as well as a sound mind, you can achieve your goals, but one without the other won't make it. This is as true today as when Juvenal wrote it nearly 1,900 years ago.

All seniors, I think, should take this saying to heart. When you were young, your body and mind were naturally efficient. However, the older you get, the more the body and mind will deteriorate unless you're prepared to work at strengthening them.

To achieve Juvenal's ideal in middle and later age takes effort in three main areas. You must: 1. Follow a good diet, so that the body is fueled efficiently and well; 2. Develop and stay with an exercise program, so that your body remains sound in wind and limb; and 3. Exercise your mind, so that it can help you reach your goals.

Let's go into these three areas now in more detail.

CHAPTER THIRTEEN

# BE SENSIBLE ABOUT DIET

**M**OST PEOPLE KNOW ME as a person who takes great pride in keeping trim and fit. They also know I'm into health foods and have read articles, say, about my sipping honey on the course or eating a handful of raisins. They can see I haven't put on weight over the years. In fact, to tell you the truth, the reverse is true. Back in 1962, I weighed 160 pounds (at 5'7"). At that time, I made a personal vow that twenty-five years later, my weight would not have increased more than five pounds. Actually, I did better than that. Today, I'm 152 pounds! So, it's no surprise that, besides my new "Walk-Through" swing, one of the hottest topics of conversation when I'm playing in pro-ams on the Senior PGA Tour or on one of my "company" days is my diet.

The seniors I talk to want answers—when do I eat, what do I eat, and what do I avoid. Do I follow a special diet? Knowing the amount I travel, many also ask me what I do to overcome the problems of jet lag. Most of them don't like what they see in the mirror every morning—too big a tummy, or too much weight around the hips. Sadly, for every senior I see who has kept his or her figure, there are dozens who are overweight. However, to a man—or woman—*they don't know what to do to get lasting results.*

There's no doubt about it: Diet today can be a very confusing subject. All of us are bombarded with seemingly contradictory data. At one moment, we hear of a report that a high fat diet cures cancer. The next, we're told that a high chloresterol level can lead to heart attacks. Then, there are all those fad diets:

> **Seniors: See your doctor before you try *any* diet. Some "fad" diets could be harmful to your health.**

water diets, melon only diets, all red meats and salad diets, high carbohydrate diets, and so on. Every one of them promises to give you back your youthful figure in a matter of weeks.

How can these diets all be good? What's a person to do?

I think the first thing to do is to take a deep breath, relax, and think about the subject sensibly.

I'm not a great believer in following the latest "fad" diet. All of us have had friends who have gone on such diets. What happens? They sometimes lose weight in the short term, but they never stick to the diet for very long. A few months, sometimes only weeks, later they go back to the way they used to eat, and all the weight comes back.

Some of these diets are actually injurious to health. If you examine them sensibly, you can see that they can't possibly supply the nutrients the body needs. You lose weight, but the wrong sort of weight—muscle instead of fat. With the most extreme diets, you could become quite ill. Moral: You should *always* talk to your doctor before going on any diet. Most doctors I've talked to emphasize one simple rule of thumb: If the diet sounds too good to be true, it invariably is!

What you need to do is follow what has proven successful and that's a sensible diet, plus exercise. Although I'll get into exercise later, I think I must mention this much now. Diet by itself won't tone up your muscles or keep you fit and strong. It's merely *one part* of keeping fit.

## THE SCALE DOESN'T LIE

THERE'S no question in my mind that the No. 1 fault in diet is simply overeating.

Strip and get on your bathroom scale. If you're ten, fifteen, or more pounds heavier than you were when in your twenties, then you're overeating. Now take a good look at yourself in a full length mirror. Look at your tummy—in profile and not "sucked in!" Honestly now, is it too big? If the answer's yes, then you're overeating. Remember: The two most faithful friends you have are your scale and mirror. They will never lie to you.

When I say "overeating," I mean that you're eating too much, considering your present level of activity. When you were younger, you had more energy, were more active. Your activity demanded more carbohydrates, for example, but you burned them up with no problem. However, now you're older, you must recognize that you're a little or a lot less active. You simply don't burn up the excess calories. The result: fat.

Put another way, I'm saying that a certain quantity of food has become a habit for you, almost a drug. As a child, you were probably conditioned to eat "three square meals" every day. In many cases, you also acquired the habit of having "seconds"— what could be called the "growing boy or girl syndrome"! As you reach senior status, you must examine such habits critically, and instill new ones. You've got to control how much you eat and also when you eat it.

As a general rule, you should put food in your body at the times of day when you're most active, not when you're resting. A saying that sums this up very nicely, I think, is: "Breakfast like a king, lunch like a prince, but dine like a pauper." In this way, your activity during the day will burn up the food. Another way of looking at it is this: Your body is much like a motor car. If you're going on a long journey, then you put gas in the car. If the car is sitting in the garage, it doesn't need any gas.

Back home on my ranch Blair Atholl in South Africa, our foreman and my close friend, Willie Betha, is living proof of the value of sensible eating combined with good, hard physical exercise. Willie has worked on the ranch for over fifty years. He starts at 6:30 A.M., has a hearty breakfast at nine, a good lunch at midday, but a small dinner in the evening. He eats much less than most "big city people," yet he can work ten times as hard. I'm many years his junior—he's at least sixty-five today and I reached my fiftieth birthday in 1985—and I have kept myself pretty fit, yet I have a tough time keeping up with him!

---

**Seniors: Eat when you're hungry, not because it's "time!" There's no rule that says you must eat three meals a day.**

In contrast, the way many older businessmen approach food, it's little wonder they're overweight. At one business meeting I recently attended, dinner was both copious and very rich. When I came down the next morning for the first meeting of the day, I still felt stuffed from the night before. So, I decided to skip breakfast. However, one of the gentlemen there, who was thirty pounds overweight if he was an ounce, loudly asked, "What's for breakfast? What's for breakfast?" He then proceeded to demolish huge quantities of bacon and fried eggs, with home fries on the side, to say nothing of buttered toast and jam, and coffee laced with cream and sugar! It was almost as though he was scared to miss a meal! Talk about poor mental conditioning!

What I'd like you to do is adopt a commonsense approach to the amount of food you eat. If you've had a huge dinner the night before, then skip breakfast altogether. Believe me, you won't die! If you can see and feel that you've put on weight because of too many business lunches and dinners during the week—and this can happen to me on occasion just as it happens to you—then fast on the Saturday. For that day, give your stomach a complete rest and drink only fruit juices and water.

*Willie Betha, the foreman at Gary Player's ranch in South Africa, is living proof of the value of sensible diet and hard exercise. As Gary says, "He's at least fifteen years my senior, but I have a tough time keeping up with him!"*

You'll find that a one day fast—something I learned from yoga —has a marvellously cleansing effect on the whole system. I highly recommend it. Then, have only two meals a day for a while until your weight returns to normal. In fact, you may well find that you only need two meals a day much of the time. I often do this, only adding a piece of fruit between the meals.

It's worth pointing out that dogs and cats normally have only one meal a day, and they thrive on it. So, don't fear you'll fade away on two—especially if you don't exercise!

When I'm playing the Senior Tour, I usually stick to two meals a day—breakfast and dinner—because obviously I'm playing golf in between. Funnily enough, I feel so fit and strong on those two meals, it's unbelievable. This is so despite the fact that I often can't get the good things I like to eat, such as good, brown, whole grain bread and fresh fruit. When I'm at home I can get the finest natural foods in the world, yet, I have to admit, I often don't feel as energetic as when I'm on tour. The only reason I can think of is that I tend to eat far too much when I'm at home—I tend to add that third meal. I'm going to have work on that!

Above all else, learn to "listen" to your body. Don't eat because "it's time." Eat because you're hungry. If you're not hungry, then don't eat!

Another major cause of obesity is eating too fast. If you eat too quickly, you don't thoroughly chew your food, and you'll eat far more than the body needs at that particular time. Also, food that hasn't been properly chewed weighs heavily on the stomach and intestines. If you don't chew your food enough, it becomes indigestible, causing stomach problems.

What you have to do is train yourself to chew each mouthful of food until it liquifies. Keep your food in the mouth as long as possible so as to allow the saliva to act on it. Savor every mouthful of food—move it around the mouth with the tongue. If you do this, you'll find you're satisfied with far less food than before.

Just as important, thorough chewing sends the food to the stomach at the right temperature and predigests the food from 50 to 75 percent depending on the thoroughness with which you chew. Digestion accounts for some 60 percent of available nervous energy. By assisting in the work of the alimentary canal, you actually free reserves of energy for other activities, including your golf!

If you want to play well, then you must apply the same sort of common sense to the timing and amount of food you eat before your round. I can't tell you the number of times I've gone to a pro-am or a business outing, and watched golfers who are old enough to know better stuff themselves with huge quantities of food from a buffet immediately before the round. They go back for "seconds," even "thirds!" Then, they wonder why they don't play well!

When you eat such a large meal just before your round, all the blood goes to your stomach and you feel very sluggish. Also, if your stomach is distended, it's impossible to turn fully —and there goes your long game! Ideally, always try to eat no less than an hour and a half before your round. Then, you'll give yourself a chance to play up to your potential.

If you know that you're in for a long day on the course—say, because of crowded conditions—then take a leaf out of my book and put some fruit in your bag to keep you going.

## FOODS I DO EAT

I don't follow a special diet. I believe in eating well, but staying away from fatty foods and too much sugar. I prefer to eat "clean" foods, those that provide energy, and keep the system in good order. I stay away from "dirty" foods that are either difficult to digest or cause one to put on weight.

The types of foods I like to eat include: high fiber foods that provide good roughage, such as whole grain bread, cereal and fruits; poultry (white meat) and fish; salads; raw or lightly steamed vegetables, such as cabbage, cauliflower, spinach, and carrots; and baked potatoes. I drink decaffeinated coffee, and Red Bush, a special herbal tea that is tannin and caffeine free. I also drink lots of water, including two glasses when I rise in the morning, and one glass before going to bed.

Incidentally, the type of water you drink is very important. For example, a scientific study showed that in Scotland, there's a larger percentage of people who have heart attacks than in London, England. This is because there's more calcium and phosphorus in the water around London. Another example is the area where I raise my horses in South Africa. We don't have a dentist in town. He'd starve. I've met fifty-year-old locals who have had, maybe, one cavity in their lives! Again, this is due to the water's high calcium/phosphorus content.

What's good for teeth is also good for the horses' bones—because of the high quality of the grazing grass. We recently ran compression tests on the bones of horses raised in our area versus those of horses raised in areas where the water (and grass) is more acid. We found that the bones of the horses raised in our area were very much the stronger.

Granted, many of you may not be able to control the type of water you drink. Nonetheless, I think water is a topic about that we all will be reading much more in the near future.

I also pay a lot of attention to how my food is prepared. My three rules in this regard are: 1. Raw fruit and vegetables are better than cooked. 2. Less cooking is better than more. 3. Broiled is better than fried.

In many ways, I've modeled my diet on that of my African friends. This is because I believe that you should always go with what has proved successful. Willie Betha, for example, has kept himself in great shape. He eats whole grain bread, raw vegetables, fruit, chicken, a little fish, and lots of water. His diet also includes mealie meal (a porridge made of corn grits). I enjoy mealie meal so much, I often take some on the road with me. With that, and my herbal tea, it's a real touch of home.

One of my favorite breakfasts is made up of raw oats, raisins, sliced bananas, nuts, wheat germ, orange juice and yogurt mixed in a bowl. That combination might not appeal to everyone, but I love it, and it works for me because these are all energy-producing foods. As I've said, on a golf day I usually skip lunch, then have an evening meal after I exercise. This might be chicken, say, with some vegetables followed by fruit, or if I'm really hungry, I might have a big salad, but with little or no dressing other than a squeeze of lemon.

# FOODS I AVOID

THE foods I avoid for the most part include: fried or fatty foods, such as pork, bacon, butter, cream, sour cream—these can make you fat and take away energy; refined sugar; tea and coffee; "junk" foods such as white bread and pastries; red meat, which is very indigestible; ice cream, desserts, and other sweets. As I've mentioned, I don't use salad dressings, because they're so fattening. I also don't add salt to my food—there's enough salt in the food I eat. I also stay away from adding anything to a baked potato, a marvellous vegetable as long as you don't load it with butter, sour cream, and bacon bits; unfortunately this is a time-honored custom in the U.S.!

I feel very strongly about fried foods. Again, I go with successful people. Leroy "Satchel" Paige, a successful pitcher in baseball at such an advanced age he had to take off a few years for publication, said that his first rule of longevity as an athlete was: "Avoid fried meats. They anger the blood." Absolutely right. I would also note that Willie Betha seldom eats fats or bacon.

I think that habit, even tradition, can be held accountable for much of the fatty foods eaten. Bacon and fried eggs is a traditional breakfast in both the U.S. and Britain, and that is usually followed by buttered toast and either jam or marmalade, washed down with either coffee or tea, cream, and white sugar. The British also love their fried fish and chips. However, if you stop to think about it, there's no *rule* that says you have to eat these foods.

One thing I know: If you want to stay fit, stay away from fried or fatty foods as much as possible.

It's interesting that, until after World War II, one seldom saw a fat Japanese. This was due to their traditional diet, which included fish, steamed vegetables, and unpolished rice. Basically it was a low fat diet. However, after the war, the Japanese imported a lot of Western food. As a result, they've increased in size, but so has their incidence of heart attacks.

In Africa, the same type of thing has happened. I've read some of the works of one expert, Professor Kloppers, who found that, in the country, blacks still have a sound diet, such as I outlined above. As a result, the incidence of heart trouble is very low, and cancer of the colon is very rare. However, the blacks who have come into the towns have taken to the white man's diet and, sadly, their health already has deteriorated.

Many of you may question my preference for herbal tea, with no tannin or caffeine over regular tea, or decaffeinated coffee over regular coffee. However, I feel that it is a factor in keeping my nerves in good condition and helping me sleep well. One may be able to tolerate coffee and tea when young, but as we

---

**Seniors: Don't be a martyr to your diet. If you crave chocolates, as I do sometimes, have a few—just compensate for them by doing some extra exercise!**

get older, I think one should take every step that will avoid broken sleep, which I know afflicts many seniors. When I think of all the coffee and tea some people drink, it does seem an awful lot of tannin and caffeine to put into the system.

As for my preference for honey over refined sugars, I can't recommend honey too highly to all seniors. First, honey doesn't need to be digested; this has been done in the stomach of the honey bee. Second, honey is a mild laxative—take too much of it, and you will soon see this effect. You should then adjust the amount you take until it's right for you. Third, honey also has a mild sedative effect, quieting the body and giving good, sound sleep.

Honey is also an excellent food supplement, being a source of vitamins as well as minerals and enzymes. It contains vitamins $B_1$, $B_2$, $B_6$ and C, as well as pantothenic acid and niacin. The minerals in honey are just as important as the vitamins. They are potassium, sodium, calcium, magnesium, iron, copper, chlorine, manganese, sulphur, and silica. These minerals are essential for body health, and need to be replaced constantly. Honey provides one with the simplest ways of getting them into the body. The enzymes in honey are also important. These enzymes are present in the digestive juices, and so honey aids digestion.

The older I get, the more I appreciate the value of honey. I know that, if you give it a chance, you will, too. Besides its health-giving qualities, honey is simply delicious! You also can get so many different kinds, you'll never become bored with it.

Having said this reminds me that one must never become a martyr to one's diet. I love chocolates! How's that for an admission from a so-called health nut! However, what I do is keep them as occasional rewards. Then, since I've indulged myself, I make up for it by extra exercise! I urge you to follow a similar plan. Don't get so darned serious about your diet that you forget to have a little fun from time to time. I'll *occasionally* have red meat, say, once every ten days or so, or even more rarely, bacon and eggs for breakfast. The trick is to do it very, very seldom, not every day.

I should also add that these are my personal preferences developed after much trial and error. Although most of what I've said will probably suit you well, if something doesn't work for you, *then chuck it out*, and experiment until you find what is best for you. As I said earlier, listen to *your* body.

A great example of this is my friend Chi Chi Rodriguez. He

happens to disagree with my feelings about red meats. As he points out, the tiger eats red meat and is pretty successful! So, Chi Chi emulates him. I must say, Chi Chi's track record speaks for itself.

## TRAVEL TRICKS

ONE of the prices I've paid for wanting to stay in my home-land, South Africa, and "commuting" to work in the U.S., Europe, the Far East and other parts of the globe is that, since 1955, I've traveled some six and a half million miles, much of it in the air. I come to the U.S. alone about six times a year. As I said earlier, it recently was calculated that I've sat in an airplane for 2.7 years! I suppose that if anyone knows how to cope with jet lag, it should be me.

I should make one point going in. No one gets used to travelling across time zones. In fact, the more you do, the worse it gets.

I recently had a dramatic example of this in my own life. When I won the U.S. Senior in July of 1987, there's no doubt that I played some of the best golf of my career. My total score of 270, fourteen under par, was nine strokes better than the record 279 set by Dale Douglass only the year before. My winning margin of six strokes over Doug Sanders, the runner-up, was two strokes better than the previous best, which was set in 1980 and matched in 1982 and 1985. However, Vivienne and I then had to rush off to the British Open that started three days later.

To get on that plane, and have to cope with the time change —five hours—was bad enough. However, I also had to adjust from the hot, sunny, humid weather in Connecticut to the gray, cold weather, and rain in Britain. I did this sort of thing as a young man, and how I ever did it, I don't know.

I went over to Britain, as you might imagine, brimming with

Seniors: When you fly, get plenty of sleep on the plane, eat fruit, and drink plenty of water. Arm yourself with tablets to combat jet lag. On arrival, immediately get on local time.

confidence in my game, and feeling that nothing could stop me from winning the championship. However, the combination of jet lag, the change in weather, and, I fear, age, caught up with me. I just wasn't myself in the British Senior. In fact, I was completely useless! From playing as well as I ever have in my life, overnight my game sank to that of a four- or five-handicapper!

The experience made me realize that, at my age, I just can't expect to get on a plane, cross umpteen time zones and go straight out on a golf course and shoot subpar golf! Nowadays, I do feel rather washed out on arrival and need about ten days to be in top form again. I think all seniors should bear this in mind when planning their itineraries.

However, while you can't totally eliminate jet lag, there are ways in which you can counteract its effects to some extent. You can help yourself, or you can make jet lag far worse than it needs to be. Over the years, I've made quite a study of it.

Of one thing I'm certain: If you're a person who can sleep well anywhere, you have a tremendous advantage. I'm fortunate, because, when I step into an airplane, I want to sleep.

What I used to do was ask the person in the same row of seats as myself, "Would you like the seats?" He invariably said, "Yes," and I would sleep on the floor, literally at his feet. Even today, I like to sleep on the floor at home or in hotels, as it helps to keep the back straight, and, as everyone knows, a golfer's back—especially as he or she gets older—is precious. However, on airplanes today, the flight attendants often don't allow me to sleep on the floor for safety reasons, so I've had to become equally adept at sleeping in my chair. Immediately my head hits the pillow, I'm gone!

On long journeys, I spend most of the time asleep. Very often, the attendant wakes me up and asks me if I'm feeling okay. Evidently, someone has said to them that I might be dead!

Above all else, avoid the "program" that the airline offers to its passengers to pass the time. This consists of, say, cocktails during the first hour, then a meal, then a film. *Don't do this.* Instead, do as I do—tell the attendant what you want to do when you board the plane, take an eyeshade with you, and get your head down!

On airplanes, most people pass the time by drinking too much alcohol, eating the wrong things, and/or smoking. I would hate to arrive feeling as dreadful as many of them must. If you stop to think about it, you know that, on arrival, your stomach won't be the same, because of changes in food and water, so why not give it an easy time?

The best thing to eat is fruit. I often take dried fruit along with me as it's easy to handle. If you want to eat something more substantial, then at least make it high fiber, like a good, whole grain bread. Avoid heavy foods, red meats and any junk food. The best thing to drink is water—lots of it. In a pressurized cabin, you become dehydrated, so water is most important.

Over the years, I've found it is helpful to take a lot of vitamin C when flying. Today, however, I take tablets specifically formulated to combat jet lag. The ones I use come from American Biosearch of San Diego, CA. You can find them at airport or hotel shops. Besides vitamins C and $B_6$, these tablets—called Anti-Jet-Lag formula—contain two natural amino acids. The folks at American Biosearch tell me our bodies use one amino acid, derived from protein, during the day to stimulate wakefulness, and the other, derived from carbohydrate, in the evening to promote sleep. Taking the daytime tablets in the morning and at lunch, and the bedtime tablets before retiring helps one adjust to the new zone.

These tablets really work! I've noticed a definite improvement in how I feel on arrival and in the first few days after that.

When you get to your destination, the most important rule is not to sleep. Instead, get on the local time immediately. In fact, you should prepare yourself mentally for this by changing your watch to the local time while you're still on the plane, say, a couple of hours before arrival on a very long flight, or even as you take off on a shorter flight. At any rate, when you arrive you must pretend that you're having a normal day on local time.

When I arive at my hotel, I find it very helpful to soak in a hot tub, and finish off with a cold shower. This gets the circulation going. I then go immediately to the golf course and practice. I find that getting fresh air into the lungs, getting the blood moving with some exercise, and, as I've said, getting on local time are the most important things to accomplish.

For you, the exercise might be going for a good walk, doing your exercises or even having a massage. But, however you do it, get on the local time and get your blood circulating! By the time you go to bed, you want to be "nicely" tired so that you go to sleep immediately. That first night's sleep is essential.

I will have a normal evening meal that evening, except that

it has to be high carbohydrate/low protein, such as pasta with no meat, because eating high protein foods would block the effect of the sleep-inducing amino acids in the nighttime "Anti-Jet-Lag" tablets. Eating carbohydrates enhances their effect. I also make sure I get plenty of roughage. This means a breakfast that includes all bran cereal, prunes, or other fruit. This is especially important for the first couple of days.

In concluding this chapter I can't let the opportunity pass without talking a little about drinking and smoking.

In a profession like mine, which involves hitting a still ball in an atmosphere of great tension, good nerves are essential. Therefore, although I'll occasionally have a beer or whisky, especially if it would be impolite to refuse, I stay away from alcohol as much as possible. However, I'm not a fanatic about it and, certainly, I've got nothing against people who drink in moderation. I recall that Harry Vardon, on being approached by a woman who wanted him to take the pledge, replied: "Moderation is essential in all things, madame, but never in my life have I failed to beat a teetotaler!" In fact, there's apparently some scientific evidence to the effect that *moderate* drinkers may live longer than those who don't drink at all.

However, as far as I know, no one can make the same claim for smoking. There's no such thing as "moderate" smoking. As one of the compulsory warnings on the side of cigarette packs puts it: "Smoking causes lung cancer, heart disease, emphysema, and may complicate pregnancy." Another one puts its more positively: "Quitting smoking now greatly reduces serious risks to your health." Think about that. I would really commend this latter thought to all seniors who are presently smokers.

We are all mortal, but to die from self-inflicted disease is something that is avoidable. Having seen many seniors struggle with quitting cold turkey, I should mention that, today, *your doctor can prescribe tablets specifically formulated to help you over the pangs of nicotine withdrawal.* That's wonderful news for smokers who up until now have found their addiction to nicotine so difficult to overcome. Today, there is help available, so go to your doctor.

With all the damning evidence against smoking, there's never been a better time to quit.

CHAPTER FOURTEEN

# EXERCISE—THE FOUNTAIN OF YOUTH

I'M NOT SURE WHO SAID, "Whenever I have the urge to exercise, I lie down until the feeling passes!" I guess there will always be some people who feel that way. However, speaking as a confirmed fitness enthusiast, I know that the saying, while very witty, was all wrong on this issue of exercise.

If there is a fountain of youth, it has to be exercise. The converse is also true. If you don't do any exercise, you're going to cut a pretty flabby figure in this world.

Generally speaking, there's nothing sadder than looking at champion boxers, baseball or football players, or other athletes ten years after their retirement. There are a few notable exceptions, of course, such as ex-world heavyweight boxing champion Floyd Patterson, who has kept himself in great shape and is a marvellous example to the young. However, in so many cases, they've let themselves go physically to the point where you barely recognize them. The same applies to so many seniors with whom I play golf. They've let themselves go to where good golf is certainly more difficult, if not impossible.

If you have a big belly, it becomes all too easy to adopt poor posture at address. Instead of standing up to the ball with the back straight, and the arms hanging from the shoulders, you're likely either to stand too erect with the hands too far from the body or reach for the ball too much with a convex curve to the back. The first puts the weight too much on the heels, the second, on the toes. Either way, you're out of balance, and your legs won't work properly during the swing. Worse, a big belly tends to put the lower spine in an unnatural, very concave position. This is because, whether standing or walking, most overweight people tend to thrust the tummy forward to balance themselves more easily. Such poor posture can lead to back problems.

If you let yourself go, you put on weight: Without exercise, your strength and flexibility will suffer, your swing will shorten, and you won't hit the ball as far.

If you want to maintain your golf ability, or improve it, you've got to exercise. Because I'm fit, I can practice longer. I've retained the same length of swing as when I was younger, and I can still hit the ball much the same distance. Because I do stretching exercises, I'm not sore after a round. Because I've kept my legs in good shape, I can still use the wider stance I described earlier as being a part of the "young man's swing"—I have no problem getting my weight back and through the ball. I can still walk even a hilly course, and not be out of wind as I come up the eighteenth hole. My energy level is high. This is all due to exercise.

Besides wanting to retain my strength and flexibility for golf, I have three other strong motivations to exercise.

First, I strongly believe in the Bible saying that one's body is a temple. I think it's up to us to make our body last as long as possible, and the only way to do that is to exercise regularly. It's a well known fact that, even if one's confined to one's bed by illness for only a few days, the muscles weaken. As the saying goes, "Rest is rust." Reg Park, a former Mr. Universe, put it this way to me one time, "I still get up at five o'clock every morning and exercise, because strength is something you have to maintain—your strength deteriorates if you leave it alone."

Second, I look at my body much as one would an investment in stocks or real estate. If I exercise, there'll be returns on that investment, besides the more obvious golf benefits. Recently, my wife Vivienne and I went to visit my daughter Teresa at the School of Arts in Winston-Salem, NC. When we arrived, there were no porters to carry the luggage, and we had three heavy pieces of baggage. So, I took them out of the car myself, and carried them up the stairs to our room. No problem. That was a return on my investment. If you look at your body in this way, you'll see that the bottom line to regular exercise is that you can do so many more things you couldn't do before.

Third, I find that fear is a very powerful motivator. I'm scared of being fat, which would not only hurt my swing and stamina, it would put me at greater risk of a heart attack. As I've told you, I'm in the horse business back in South Africa. I don't see any fat horses winning races! In fact, there's a saying, "The longer the race, the leaner the horse." I've become a little leaner as I get older, and, from what I hear from doctors, that's healthy. I don't think that you seniors should fear losing a little weight as you get older, rather the reverse. We're all in a race to prolong our useful lives. Let's stay lean and keep running as long as we can!

I think all of you should consider these points. Everyone likes to see women and men who have kept their figures and fitness. So, why not set a good example? If you invest time in your body, you'll find it's the one investment that makes all others have meaning; without your health and strength, you have nothing, even if you're as rich as Croesus. Also, the more exercise you take and the trimmer you are, the less likely you are to have heart troubles. Good diet helps, but the ultimate answer is not only to eat less, but exercise more!

Of course, there's always the wise guy who says, "Well, if exercise is so good for you, what about Jim Fixx, the famous runner, who died young?!" My answer is that there will always be people like Fixx whose families have histories of heart disease. So, having the right genes is important. However, to take unfortunate examples like that and make them excuses for not doing any exercise is a cop out. All doctors agree that, to enjoy the best of health, you must exercise. However, they do advise having a physical examination before beginning an exercise program.

Exercise gives you many rewards. I know that when I'm fit, my reflexes and touch are better, my eyesight is sharper, as is my hearing. Just as important, my brain is clearer and my concentration is keener. A little known fact is that exercise makes the bones big and strong as well as toning or building muscle —an important factor as one gets older. All this may sound almost too good to be true, but I assure you it isn't.

## PICKING YOUR PROGRAM

I wouldn't presume to dictate to you exactly what exercises you should perform. Actually, I really shouldn't, because, in so many ways, it's a matter of "horses for courses." A person who

> **Seniors: Running on a hard surface can injure your back and knees. Go for a walk instead.**

is slim and flexible like Don January, for example, has different needs from someone who is overweight. What suits a person of fifty may not suit one of seventy, and so on.

However, when planning your exercise program, you should bear in mind that the ideal figure for a golfer is that of the popular cartoon character, Popeye. He has a thin neck, a flat chest, small biceps, immensely strong forearms, wrists, and hands, a narrow waist with a flat stomach, but big, strong thighs and calves. This means that, for golf, never attempt to develop the shoulders, chest, or biceps to where you add a lot of bulk. In the 1960s—and I shudder when I think of it—some golf coaches were telling their young golfers to get on their backs and do bench presses. They developed bulk in the shoulders, chest and biceps—and ruined their golf games.

In general, you need to do some aerobic exercise, something to get the heart pumping, and the blood coursing through the veins. You also need to do some stretching exercises, and some exercises to maintain or build muscle. It's worth pointing out that some people, like myself, have the ability to relax instantly. Others are very stiff or tense, and need exercises that give maximum stretching, then relaxation of the muscles. While I'll discuss my own program, I'll also discuss alternatives, as well as supplementary exercises.

Before I get to my own program, let me dispose of two types of exercise—running (or jogging) and weight lifting—that so many seniors ask me about. They know that I've done plenty of both in my time and wonder whether they are essential or even desirable. Well, I would never want to discourage very keen, fit people from either activity, but otherwise, the answer is usually no to both. Here's why.

Running is a marvellous aerobic exercise, one that exercises the whole body. If you start when young and stay with it, there's no question you'll control your weight and reduce your chances of heart trouble. When I was younger, I did a lot of running. However, I found it does have a down side. When you get older, the jarring effect running has on your body is very bad for you. When I see seniors pounding along a concrete sidewalk or road, my heart bleeds for them. I've been there, and know they're asking for knee as well as back trouble—there's no doubt in my mind that running contributed to my back problems. That's why today I usually use an exercycle—an aerobic exercise that doesn't have these harmful side effects.

I'm not going to say don't run. However, if you're forty years old or over, and have never run, I don't think this is the time to start. Far better you go for a good, brisk walk on the days you don't play golf. However, if you decide to run anyway, never run on hard surfaces or along busy roads, where you're breathing in a lot of carbon monoxide. Run on grass or a good indoor track with some spring to it. That's just common sense.

The same thinking applies to weight lifting. If you're under forty, are extremely fit, and have always worked out with weights, then you can certainly continue at fifty, sixty, or even older. In my travels, I find that more and more hotels have gyms equipped with the latest in free weight, Universal, or Nautilus equipment, and I'll take advantage of it. So can you, if you've always been a keen weight lifter. However, if you're forty years or older, and have never lifted weights, this is not the moment to start.

My own program today consists of what I call "convenience exercises." All of them can be done at home, and the needed equipment is easy to acquire. I really think this is the best course for most seniors, for several reasons.

First, if you have all the equipment ready at hand, you're far more likely to exercise than if you have to go to a gym. Second, home exercises are usually easier to fit into your schedule. Third, going to a gym for someone who is out of shape can be a traumatic experience. You feel self-conscious parading that fat tummy or thick hips, and who needs that? At home, you don't have this problem.

I would stress that there's no one best time of day to exercise. I like to exercise after my round in the afternoon, or early evening, before I have my bath and evening meal. This is because I'm so much looser than in the morning. In the afternoon, for example, I can lie on my back on the floor with my

---

**Seniors: Make up a wall chart listing your exercise program. It's a wonderful motivational tool.**

legs together, then bring them over my head until they touch the floor. In the morning, I can only get the feet to a point a couple of inches above the floor. However, suit yourself. If you prefer to rise early and exercise in the morning, that's fine. The point is to make the time to exercise, period.

I exercise for one hour five days a week. However, if you are just starting to exercise, fifteen or twenty minutes, perhaps three days a week, will be enough. You can always increase the time—and the number of exercises you do—later, as you get fitter and stronger. That's why I've deliberately given you a lot of exercises to choose from. I don't expect or want you to plunge into all of them. As a minimum, I'd like you to select one exercise from the aerobic section, say the exercycle, the exercises with the heavy club, and some other exercises from the stretching section, and at least the situps and one of the forearm/hand exercises from the strengthening section. If I could get every senior to do that, I'd be happy. However, remember, that is just a start! Always keep setting your goals higher!

All successful people, whether they're business people or homemakers, make up lists of "Things to do." Such a list helps you have the discipline to actually get these things done. This is also an excellent plan to follow when exercising.

Make up a nice, big, neat chart of the exercises you're going to do, head it "My Exercise Program," and display it prominently on a wall of the room in which you'll exercise. One way to organize it is to list the exercises in columns across the top of the page, and the days of the week down the left hand side. Then, if you take a ruler, you can create boxes in which you can note the amount of time you devote to, say, the exercycle, and the number of repetitions with other exercises. As you increase the time and repetitions, use a *different color* pen to show your new figures. Then, you have a nice "visual" of your progress and that provides you with renewed motivation. You can also note your weight and other vital statistics at the start of the program, and periodically note improvements. When you reach the end of your first chart, file it and make out another, and keep going. From time to time, get out that first chart and compare the figures with where you are now. You'll feel good to see the results of your efforts, and it will inspire you to greater heights.

I always exercise to music, and I think you'll find this useful, too. Select music that's appropriate to the type of exercise you're doing. For example, when cycling, select music with a brisk tempo. When doing stretching exercises, choose something with a slower beat, and so on.

Always use common sense when you exercise. If, for example, you've done some vigorous aerobic exercise that day, such as swimming, then you don't need to cycle during your exercise program. Skip the aerobics and start with stretching. If you have used your hands and forearms vigorously all day, say, in a carpentry project, then later you should leave out exercises for the hands and forearms, and so on.

A good rule is to *always* listen to your muscles as you exercise. Do a particular exercise until the muscles complain, then, depending on the type of exercise, at the very most continue for a few more seconds or do just one or two more repetitions, then quit. *Increase the time you devote to an exercise, or the number of repetitions, very, very gradually. You may stay with the same regimen days at a time until your body tells you you're ready to move along a step and move up.*

Don't worry too much if you fail to exercise one day. *Just get back on the program tomorrow!* Remember: It took a long time for you to get used to not exercising. You must have patience with yourself when establishing a new habit. As any psychologist will tell you, it does take time.

However, once exercise has become a habit, you'll find it has rewards you never dreamed of. I come back from the golf course some days—and we've all had such days!—and the last thing I feel like doing is to exercise. But I say to myself, "No pain, no gain!" And after I've exercised, I feel a new man. Like me, you'll find that regular exercise renews your body, your whole spirit. That's a promise!

## GET THE BLOOD PUMPING

I begin my workout on the exercycle. I myself pedal for about twenty-five minutes, and work up a good sweat. When you start, don't discourage yourself by setting the tension on the cycle so high that you're winded within a couple of minutes. Set the tension low so that you can keep going longer. What you want to do is to get the heart pumping vigorously. So, a couple of minutes' exercise is not enough, but twenty-five at the beginning is probably too much. You might start with ten minutes. Later, when you become fitter, you can gradually increase the minutes and the tension so that you're strengthening the legs as well.

My own exercycle, by the way, is one on which the handles are stationary, as on a regular bike. This is because I do other exercises for my arms. However, if you don't do arm exercises, then the type of exercycle on which the arms move as well as the legs could be better for you.

If you don't have an exercycle, excellent substitutes are: swimming laps, jumping rope like a boxer (on a springy floor or grass), stair climbing, or a brisk walk.

Swimming and jumping rope obviously are good exercises

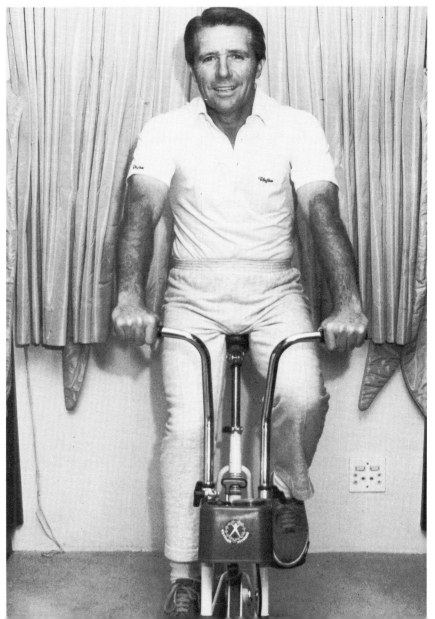

*Aerobic exercise, such as the exercycle, is an important key to fitness.*

for getting the blood moving. Stair climbing, I must admit, doesn't sound like serious exercise. However, I assure you that you can make it into a marvellous aerobic exercise in at least a couple of different ways.

First, if you live in a house with stairs, select a flight that gives you ten steps, preferably in a line. One repetition would be to walk up and down these ten steps in twelve seconds. Use a watch with a second hand so that you can time yourself. This might seem a slow pace, but don't go faster just because it appears so easy. Start off by trying for, say, five repetitions, then *very gradually* increase up to say ten or fifteen. You'll know you've had a workout, believe me!

Second, for office workers, learn to walk up to your office rather than use the elevator. Let's say that you work on the tenth floor. The first day, walk up to the second floor and take the elevator from there. The next week, walk to the third floor, and stay at that level for three weeks. Then, walk to the fourth floor, and so on. Again, a gradual increase is the key to success.

Another aerobic exercise that is apt to get overlooked is walking. If you walk briskly for a couple of miles *without stopping* on the days you don't play golf, this actually is marvellous exercise. Swinging your arms vigorously, like a race-walker, makes it even better.

It should go without saying that you should walk when playing golf. Golf, after all, has traditionally always been a walking game. However, sad to say, far too many seniors—and even youngsters—in America ride in golf carts. By so doing, they miss out on walking, one of the best and safest exercises of all. If you're unable to walk the course, that's different. Out on the Senior Tour, we have Charlie Owens, who has a fused left knee due to a parachute accident in the service, and has had several operations on his right knee. He obviously must use a cart. However, if you have no medical reason for riding, take every opportunity to walk.

My mother-in-law is seventy. She plays golf three times a week. She doesn't even know what a cart is. She always walks and is fit as a fiddle. Everywhere else in the world I've been, including Britain, Australia, and South Africa, people of all ages do the same, or they take a pull cart. Believe me, they enjoy their golf more than any cart rider, and they're far the fitter for it.

I know that some courses force you to use a golf cart. That can be a problem, but, if you plan ahead, you can still do some walking. Make an arrangement with the person sharing your cart. For example, say, "How about my walking the first nine, and you, the second nine?" If you haven't walked in a while, then build up slowly. Ride sixteen holes, and walk two holes, then ride fourteen, and walk four, and so on. At some courses that require carts you're allowed to walk the course later in the afternoon or in the evening. If this is the case at your course, then invest in a light canvas bag and play at least some of your golf walking. You'll never regret it.

I remember returning to the States in August for the 1987 GTE Northwest Classic. I came in on the weekend before the tournament. I was suffering from jet lag, and somehow I had caught a really rotten cold, but I still managed to walk the very hilly course at the Inglewood CC, Kenmore, WA. To keep going, I said to myself, "Every time they [the other competitors] ride in a cart, and you walk up those hills, that gives you strength for the future."

Tell yourself the same thing—it's really true.

## STRETCH

NEXT, I do some stretching exercises. Again, I'm not going to dictate—there's really no set way to stretch. However, stretch you must if you want to keep your suppleness and also avoid injury when you come to strength-building exercises.

I'm going to give you some of my favorites. Try them all, then select the ones that help you the most. As a general rule, do six repetitions of each stretch; do six on each side of the body on a "one-sided" stretch. When you start stretching exercises, it's a good idea to do them in front of a mirror so you can see you are doing them correctly.

I should add that some of the following are more strengthening exercises than stretching—the reason I'm including them here is that I find it convenient to do them in this order, because I'm already in the right position to do them. You may find this convenient, too, and certainly you should apply this principle when making up your own program. Obviously, it saves time.

The first one is called the Williams (see photos page 206). Start by sitting on the floor, hugging your knees. Roll back until the toes are behind the head, then roll forward to the starting position and repeat. This massages and loosens up the spine.

*The "Williams" massages and loosens up the spine.*

Then, relax for a moment lying on your back with your legs straight, the feet together, and the hands at your sides. Next, raise the legs as slowly as possible, bringing them to a vertical position. Then, by contracting the stomach muscles, bring the thighs to the chest. Toward the end of this movement, the knees can bend a little so that your knees touch the face (see photo below). Now stretch out the legs and allow the feet to sink as close to the ground as you can get them. See if you can stretch your feet a couple more inches back when you breathe out. That stretches the whole spine. Then slowly reverse the process, finishing in the starting position. This is a yoga exercise called "the plough." It works out the whole spine.

Still on your back, extend the arms straight from the shoulders in a "T" position, and then turn the hips and legs as

*The yoga "plough" exercise works out the whole spine.*

Seniors: You can help to get rid of many tension headaches by gently stretching the neck to the right and left, and forward and back, followed by very, very slow neck rolls.

much as possible to the right while keeping the shoulders and arms flat on the floor. Hold this position for a few seconds (see photo), then repeat on the left side. This gives the spine an excellent twisting stretch.

From the same starting position, another good spine twister is to swing the left leg over the right until it touches the floor, hold, and return to the starting position. Then repeat, swinging the right leg over the left (see photo below).

*This exercise gives the spine a good "twisting" stretch.*

Next, stretch out the joints of the legs by bending the left knee, and pulling the thigh into the chest, and then repeat with the right leg (see page 208).

Then go to some neck stretches. (A supple neck is essential to a golfer, because you should "hit past your chin," that is, keep your chin pointing behind the ball until the ball has gone.) You can do them in two ways.

The first way is on your back, as I'm doing in the photos on page 208, turning your neck left, and holding that position for a few seconds, then right, and hold. Then bring the head forward (sinking the chin into the chest), and hold.

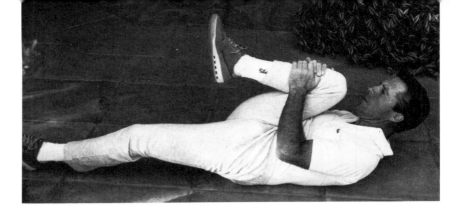

*To stretch out the knees, pull the thigh into the chest.*

*Neck stretches help a golfer to "hit past his chin."*

*This exercise stretches the upper back; is also good for the stomach muscles.*

*A similar stretch for the upper back, with a stronger effect on the stomach.*

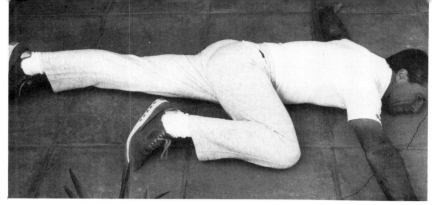

*A wonderful stretcher and strengthener of the lower back.*

The second way you can do anytime from a sitting position (not shown). It is especially useful when your neck needs a more thorough workout. When stretching your neck to the right, cup your chin in the right palm, with your fingers on your right cheek, and hold the back of the head with the left palm, the fingers along the upper right side of the head. Now, by gently pushing back with your right palm and forward with the left (both are clockwise), you can increase the stretch of the neck to the right. Reverse the hand holds and push counter-clockwise for a stretch to the left. For the forward stretch, clasp your hands on the upper back part of your head and gently pull down. You can also do a backward stretch by pressing both hands against your forehead. Incidentally, these neck stretches, along with very slow neck rolls—where you roll your head in a complete circle to the left and then to the right, that is, passing through the four positions above—will cure many a tension headache. That's another tip from yoga!

To stretch out the upper back, raise your head and feet off the ground, clasp your hands behind the neck, then bring the left knee back as far as it will go while you touch the left leg with your right elbow, and repeat on the other side. Then extend both arms and bring both knees back. This series of stretches is also marvellous for the stomach.

Now turn face downward, legs extended, feet together and put your arms out in a "T," and then alternately bend each leg, bringing the knee up toward the chest (see photo above). This stretches and strengthens the lower back.

Now here you can include an exercise called the "reverse swallow." From the face down position, you raise your feet and

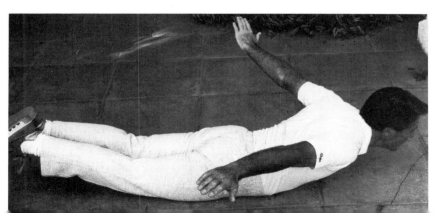

*The "reverse swallow" is a powerful lower back strengthener.*

*Side leg raises stretch the groin; tone legs, buttocks, and arms.*

legs as well as the head and shoulders from the floor with the arm extended backward and hold the position for a few seconds. This strengthens the lower back (see page 209, bottom).

Now for some side leg raises. Lying on your left side, adopt the same position shown in the above photo except that the right leg is extended and lying on the ground. Then raise the right leg as high as you can, while pushing down strongly with the right arm. Hold for a few seconds. Lower the right leg. Then lie on your right side, and reverse the starting position so you can lift the left leg. This is a marvellous stretch for the groin. It also tones and strengthens the legs, buttocks, and arms.

The next exercise can be done statically or dynamically (see photo). Statically, you start in the "up" position of a push-up,

*An excellent stretch for the legs. Can double as an aerobic exercise.*

supporting yourself with your hands beneath your shoulders and legs extended. Then bring the right knee under the chest, hold for a few seconds, then extend the right leg and bring the left knee under the chest and hold for a few seconds. This is a marvellous stretch for the legs. Done dynamically, you can also make this a terrific aerobic exercise by "running" with alternate knees going underneath the chest.

Now, from a starting position on your hands and knees, extend the right leg backward, and extend the left arm forward. Hold the position for a few seconds before returning to the starting position. Now repeat in reverse. This is another stretch I took from yoga; it does a great job of strengthening the extensor muscles in the back.

Coming to a standing position, raise the arms above the head and grasp the fingers of one hand with the other hand, feet slightly apart, as shown. Now stretch to the right and hold for a few seconds. Now return to the starting position and stretch to the left. These stretches are excellent for the spine and waist.

*Side bends are excellent for the spine and waist.*

A "late hit" exercise—pull with the left arm, resist with the right arm.

Stretching toward the toes is very good for the back.

Another stretch for the knees, also marvellous for your balance.

While you're still grasping one hand with the other, I'll throw in a dynamic tension exercise, which simulates the pulling action of the left arm in the late hit. You can't do too many exercises to train yourself to hit late! Bring the arms in front of you and, for a few seconds, pull to the left with the left arm while you resist with the right arm.

With the legs still apart, stretch the hands above your head, then turn the upper body to the right and stretch forward toward the toes as far as you can go. Repeat, stretching toward the left foot. This is great for the back.

Also, stand on the right foot, raise the left leg, and then, grasping it below the knee with the hands, pull it into the chest. Hold this position for a few seconds, then lower the left foot to the ground. Then reverse the exercise, standing on the left foot. Besides stretching the knees, this is marvellous for your balance.

## GOLF EXERCISES

EARLIER in this book, in Chapter Four, I talked about using a heavy club to ingrain the correct swing positions. I also suggested you make slow motion swings with the heavy club, starting with, say, five swings and working up to as much as ten minutes' swinging a day. I'd now like to talk about these and other golf exercises you can do from the point of view of fitness.

First of all, as a golfer, you want to develop the muscles you need for golf, but not any others. It should therefore come as no surprise that one of the best exercises for golf is the golf swing itself.

More important, a heavy club provides some of the most complete exercise you can do. Swinging the club—especially when you get up to several minutes—is really good aerobic exercise; believe me, your heart will be pumping nicely when you finish! Swinging the club is a marvellous stretching exercise and will do wonders for your flexibility. It also strengthens the golf muscles, as does posing the different swing positions.

Here I'd like to acknowledge a great debt to Henry Cotton, who, besides being a three-time British Open champion, was also a marvellous teacher. He pioneered developing the golf

*Swinging the heavy club is at once an aerobic, stretching, and strengthening exercise.*

*Single-handed swings strengthen both sides of the body as well as educating them to their tasks in the swing.*

muscles through golf exercise. Over the years, we've had some great talks on the subject.

Henry always recommended making golf swings, and hitting balls, with just the left hand on the club and then just the right hand. I thoroughly endorse this, and often hit balls this way on the range. Not only do you strengthen both sides of the body, you also *educate* them to their tasks in the golf swing. When you become strong enough, you can emulate what I'm doing in the photos, making single-handed swings with the heavy club!

If you have to exercise indoors, and don't have room to swing a club of any kind, then use a fairly heavy dumbbell or other handweight and swing that instead, as I'm doing in the photos.

*If you have no room to swing a club, swing a dumbbell or handweight instead.*

*Build up the strength of your hands and forearms by "cutting" rough.*

Henry was also a great believer in building up the strength of the hands and forearms by hitting against resistance. For example, if you have some thick, deep rough available, then go in there with an old iron and cut some grass as I'm doing in the photo. This is a terrific exercise.

One of the problems I've talked over with Henry is the "spinal sag" that afflicts any longtime golfer. Whenever I used to go to my tailor, he would keep on telling me to stand up straight. I'd reply, "I am." The problem was that I had got so used to setting up to a golf ball with the right shoulder higher than the left, my spine had taken a set in that position. To counteract this problem, Henry recommended I do what he called "contras," that is, setting up and swinging *left-handed*. This really helps. Include "contras" in your heavy club sessions.

---

**Seniors:** My back has hurt me from time to time partly due to out-of-condition stomach muscles. That's why I do 300 sit-ups a day (but not at one time!) I hear that Reggie Jackson does 500! See your doctor and ask him if this could help you.

## OTHER STRENGTH BUILDERS

YOU will have noticed that I have included many stretches and strengtheners for the back. This probably didn't surprise you, since we all know how important it is for a golfer to keep his or her back in good shape.

I'm living proof of this. At one time, I had a really bad back. I tried everything to cure it, including acupuncture, hanging up-side down, and so on. Nothing helped me until, first, I started using the "Walk-Through" swing, and second, a caddie, Nick De Paul, told me what a doctor from Philadelphia had told him. "Gary's pretty fit, but his stomach is not in as good shape as the rest of his body. If he'd work more on his stomach and lower back, the bad back would go!"

This was all I needed to hear. Now, besides my back exercises, I also do a lot of sit-ups as part of my daily exercise. Sit-ups are terrific for both reducing and strengthening the stomach and lower back. My bad back is history!

In doing sit-ups, it's a good idea to hook your feet underneath something. In the photos, I've hooked my toes under another person's boots. However, you can also hook your feet under your exercycle or a piece of furniture. Note that I am

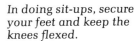

*In doing sit-ups, secure your feet and keep the knees flexed.*

*In twisting this device, you work the hands and forearms against a spring*

starting with the knees bent and keeping them bent—this is most important. Begin by doing, say, twenty sit-ups (or fewer if necessary), and gradually work up. I now do 300 a day, not all at once and not all full sit-ups, I hasten to add! I do them in blocks of fifty at various times in the day. However, don't imagine that I'm anything exceptional. Reggie Jackson, I hear, does 500 a day! And I've heard of some people who do 1,000. It's surprising what you can do if you set your goals high. At one time, I never thought I would be able to do 150, let alone 300.

If you are starting from a low level of fitness, and find the sit-up too strenuous, try the "sit-back." Anchor your feet, but start from the sitting position with the knees fully bent, and lean back halfway to the floor, hold that position a few seconds, and then sit up again.

Then, I'm a great believer in strengthening the hands and forearms. As Henry Cotton often told me, "Your hands and forearms can't be too strong for golf." Here are some other great exercises for these areas.

As you watch TV, squeeze a rubber ball, a spring grip, or mold Play Dough in your hands. You can also take a sheet of newspaper, hold a corner of it in one hand, then slowly crumple the paper into a ball. If you're strongly right-handed, remember to give your left hand extra work.

A device you can improvise at home is to tie a heavy weight to, say, a three-foot length of cord. Attach the other end of the cord to a piece of one-inch dowel and, with the arms extended, wind the weight up and down. Alternatively, if you can get the device I'm using in the photos, this is just as good. The one I have has a spring inside the handle. You twist it one way and it tightens the spring, the other way it releases the spring.

*Another exercise that helps you make the "late hit."*

Another device I have at home is a grip to which is attached a heavy rubber band. You hook the rubber band onto a doorknob, then you do a dynamic tension exercise, pulling to the left with the whole body while in the late hit position. With a little ingenuity, you can probably improvise something similar.

If you have a pair of dumbbells or similar weights, there are many strengthening exercises you can do. Do at least an equal amount of work with the weight in each hand, but, as I said before, if you're right-handed, do more with the left side. Here are some I do. Note that on exercises 1 and 4, you should use one weight, working one arm at a time. On the other two, you can, if you wish, use two weights at once.

1. Holding the weight with your elbow into your side, rotate the weight from palm up to palm down. Also, work the wrist

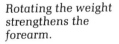

*Rotating the weight strengthens the forearm.*

*Rotating the weight strengthens the arm and deltoid.*

up and down from both a palm up and palm down position. 2. With the arm extended to the side just below shoulder level, rotate the weight from palm up to palm down. 3. With your hand at your side, raise the weight forward to just below shoulder level, then back as far as you can. 4. Lying on your stomach on a bed, with the arm you want to exercise hanging down the side of the bed, lift the weight up backwards as far as

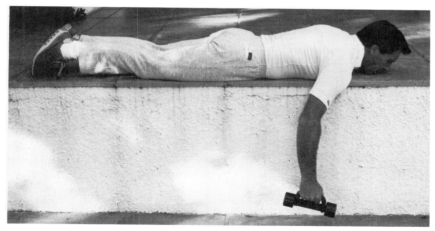

*This exercise strengthens the "lat" and your shoulder extension.*

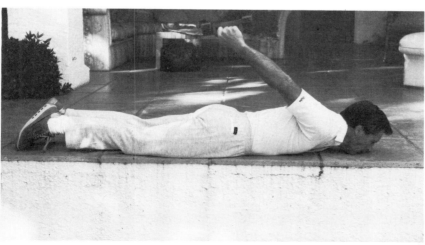

you can—this is marvellous for the "lat," the big muscle in the back below the shoulder, and your shoulder extension.

While you're on the bed, put the weight to one side, and lie face down, with one leg over the side of the bed, the foot on the ground. Now lift the leg as high as you can while keeping it extended. This is another good one for the lower back. As you become stronger, you can increase the effect of this exercise by leaving your shoes on.

For the legs, here's an exercise I've done all my life—a ski exercise. With your back to a wall and your arms at your sides, sit down, and hold the position. At first, you may not be able to get your thighs to horizontal—no matter, go down as close to it as you can. Start maybe with a twenty second hold, and work up to one minute. This is a fantastic exercise; it strengthens the quadriceps muscles at the back of the thighs.

*Caution: When you start on the exercise, make certain you have the arm of a sofa, or, say, the seat of your exercycle next to you. You can get stuck down there!*

## I CAN STILL DO THESE

BESIDES the number of sit-ups I can do and the amount of time I can "sit" in the ski exercise, I take a pride in some other exercises I can still do at fifty-plus. For example, as you can see in the photos, I still do what I call "rabbit jumps," where I jump high in the air, and turn at the same time so that I make complete circles. This, by the way, is a marvellous aerobic exercise. I can also do chin-ups, one-handed press-ups, one-legged squats, hold my heavy club in just two fingers, not using the thumb, and so on.

Although this may sound vainglorious, let me explain why I think it's a legitimate type of pride. To exercise regularly, most of us need to use any and *every* motivational tool we can lay our hands on! I think you'll find that, after you've exercised a while, you too will start to take pride in what you can do. I think this pride is all to the good, as long as you don't let it deteriorate into outright narcissism. It's fun, it's good for the ego, and, as I've said, it also provides that extra motivation to keep exercising. So, don't knock it!

Also, another "party trick" of mine—the hand stand—led me to investigate yoga.

Player can still do these at fifty-plus: A ski exercise, in which you "sit" against a wall; "rabbit jumps" in which he jumps and turns, a marvellous aerobic exercise; chin-ups in which he pulls his knees into the chest...

. . . one-handed pressups;
one-legged squats; an exercise
in which he holds his heavy
club with two fingers—no
thumb; and handstands.

## THE VALUE OF YOGA

WHEN I was a young golf professional, I used to make a little extra money by taking bets that I could "walk" around the edge of a billiard table on my hands. I've always liked to do handstands, and as you can see from the photo, I still do. I think this is what initially attracted me to yoga.

Although my handstand started as just a fun thing to do, I soon realized that it gave me great benefits. Reversing the normal position of the body sends more blood to the brain and helps it function better. Although I can't prove it, I suspect that the increased blood supply to the head also improves the sight and hearing. When I heard that yogis did something very similar, the headstand, and placed a very high value on the practice, this intrigued me.

I was not disappointed in my study of yoga. As you can see, I still do many yoga stretches and recommend them. I also suggest your investigating yoga on your own.

Here, in brief, are some other benefits of yoga. First, yoga stretches are extremely thorough. If you're a person who tends to be extremely uptight, and tense, if you come home from work in need of a good, stiff drink, then yoga stretches are for you. They'll work all the kinks out of you far better—and quicker—than alcohol, and you'll be improving your health in the bargain. Second, if you don't need to increase muscle strength, but only need to tone existing muscle and maybe work on your flexibility, then yoga stretches could be just what you need. Third, yoga deep-breathing exercises by themselves are marvellously calming.

Finally, and most important, to be able to meditate successfully, something I'll cover in the next chapter, you must be completely relaxed before you start. As I've said, I'm lucky in this respect, because I've always been able to put the tensions of the day behind me quickly, and relax completely. However, for those of you who find it difficult to relax, here's the yoga way to learn to relax.

Lie on your back on the floor. Your legs should be slightly apart, your arms extended close to your body. Close your eyes. Now stretch your right foot—really stretch hard, making the leg muscles contract, and study what is happening. Hold the stretch while you trace all the contractions that are taking place, then let the foot and leg relax. Next, repeat this process, but in slow motion. Build the stretch up very, very slowly and hold it, while keeping track of every sensation that occurs. Then, still in slow motion, let go, allowing the muscles to relax. The secret of success is to let go as slowly as possible so that you take the "let go" process beyond the point where you're conscious of any physical sensation. What you want to do is reach the stage where you're no longer *trying* to relax but simply have lost all feeling of alertness in the muscles concerned.

To relax your whole body, apply the slow motion "stretch and let go" technique to all the muscles in the body working from the feet up. In other words, you'd stretch in succession the muscles of the feet, calves, thighs, stomach, buttocks, chest, back, hands and arms, then the face.

At the end of this process, you'll no doubt be lying there more relaxed than ever before. That's the time to feel this total limpness, this total relaxation, in its entirety.

In time, you'll find you no longer have to use the "stretch and let go" technique. Instead, you can summon up this feeling of total relaxation at will.

Unfortunately, it's beyond the scope of this book to give you more than a taste of what yoga has in store for you. I just hope I've whetted your appetite.

## CHAPTER FIFTEEN

# DEVELOP MENTAL STRENGTH

A S WE GET OLDER, it's not just the body that tends to get flabby. The same problem can afflict the mind. If one had to identify mental faults that tend to afflict us seniors, he would have to include the following: becoming smug and self-satisfied; living off past accomplishments; and, indeed, living in the past generally. If you find yourself constantly talking about the "good old days," and perhaps moaning a little about your present lot, you should recognize that this has happened to you!

Now, we can't put the clock back. We are fifty years old, sixty, or whatever. However, in the same way that exercising the body can give us the characteristics of youth—energy, flexibility, and strength—so exercising the mind can keep us young in spirit.

To do this, I think we should first explore the qualities we would ideally expect to see in the young. These would include courage in the face of adversity, enthusiasm, a positive attitude, and faith in the future. Then, we can go into practical ways in which we can live these qualities, such as goal setting, visualization, concentration, meditation and self-talk.

## ADVERSITY—A GOOD TEACHER

THERE is an old Chinese proverb that says you've got to have determination to succeed in life, but in the process you must be prepared to suffer. Also, in Plutarch's *Lives*, Marcus Licinius Crassus says, "Those who aim at great deeds must also suffer greatly." Both these sayings ring very true to me. In golf and in life, nothing comes easily. I strongly believe that the ability to accept adversity and overcome it, is one of the most important virtues, because it offers us the greatest opportunities for growth.

In many ways, I think I was fortunate to grow up in poor, rather hard, circumstances, because it taught me this lesson early.

## EARLY DAYS

MY father, Harry, had to leave school when his own father died at an early age. I grew up in the Johannesburg suburb of Booysens. We lived in a poor neighborhood; our house was actually over a gold mine, called Robinson Deep, where my father was mine captain. He never made over $200 a month in his life, and that for working 12,000 feet under the ground. When I was eight, my mother died of cancer, at age forty-four.

Going to school meant rising at six o'clock. I took a trolley car into the middle of the city, then walked about three-quarters of a mile so as to take a bus out of town to King Edward VII School. The journey took an hour and a half. I did this twice a day from age seven.

An early memory of mine is that I always took off my shoes and school clothes when I got home. I had to make them last, because there was no money to replace them.

My father always said that moaning about life was absolutely of no use. No one was interested in your problems. My mother was the same way. In the closing days of her life, she would always tell people she was "just fine," or "a little better today, thank you." As she said, "People have their own problems—they don't want to hear about yours."

I also remember the early evening as being a tough, rather lonely time, as I waited for my father and sister Wilma to come

> **Seniors: Don't become a moaner. As my mother used to say, "People have their own problems. They don't want to hear about yours."**

home from work. However, I don't remember ever feeling sorry for myself. Looking back on it, I realize that this was because my father had made it abundantly clear that you must see hardships as challenges, and answer them positively.

## WHAT ADVERSITY TEACHES

MY early life was full of adversity, but thanks to my father's example, I turned it to positive advantage. It gave me the drive to succeed. I became, and still am, an extremely hard worker. I had, and still have, thank God, unbounded enthusiasm for everything I've done and do. When you come from a background like mine, you're truly thankful for the opportunity to succeed.

Of course, this progression from adversity to hard work to enthusiasm is not exclusive to me. So many people who are successful in life are those who have come from poverty. However, I must say it was a key to my development as a player and as a person.

If someone asked me the two hardest things I've had to do in my life, I'd say that, first, it would be leaving my wife, my six wonderful children, my home and my country in order to make my living. To leave your loved ones and home and go to live in a motel, and be rushing around airports, and missing flights, and the hectic pace of it all, yes, that's still one of the most difficult things for me to do. The other thing that I've found most difficult to do is my exercises. Even though I've exercised since I was fourteen years old, I still find it tough to do them—especially after a hard day of travel. However, if I ever weaken, I remind myself that nothing worthwhile is gained without sacrifice.

## BILLY GRAHAM HELPS ME

BILLY GRAHAM, the evangelist, gave me a great insight into adversity and how it fits into God's scheme for us. In fact, without this lesson, I would never have won the 1961 Masters.

I visited him in his home before I went down to Augusta. While we relaxed in his Jacuzzi, we discussed all sorts of things. He asked why I had become so successful so early in life, and I told him that I was convinced that it was all due to three of my basic beliefs: faith in God, faith in the value of education, and faith in physical fitness. He thought about that a while, then said, "I know how badly you want to win the Masters. Now, when you're playing in the tournament, I want you to thank God for all the bad shots and all the difficulties you encounter. Any man can thank God for the good things that happen to him, but very few people say 'thank you' for the lousy things."

Well, that sounded very strange to me at first. However, in the last round, I came to a crucial point in the tournament. I was four shots ahead of Arnold Palmer as I came to the thirteenth hole, but then I pushed my drive right into the pines and, what with one thing and another, took a double bogey 7 on the hole and then, on the fifteenth, missed a short putt and had to settle for a bogey 6.

I thought I had blown my lead and that, by the time Arnold played the fifteenth himself, he'd have caught me or even taken a lead over me. So I said to God, "Well, I'm grateful because now You've really given me a test. There are three holes to go: We will see if I'm up to your challenge." I had to scramble but I got pars on sixteen and seventeen, and then, as previously described, I parred eighteen as well when I got the ball up and down in two from the right trap.

The 1961 Masters was a marvellous lesson for me. If I had felt sorry for myself after taking that 7—and who among us hasn't done that sort of thing?—I would probably have lost by one or two strokes. As it was, I squeaked home a winner.

It is an experience that has stood me in good stead from that day to this. It taught me always to try to take adversity on the chin, and use it positively to strengthen myself for future endeavors.

People always talk about my match in 1965 with Tony Lema in the semifinals of the World Match Play championship at Wentworth, England, It *was* an incredible match. I was one up after nine, six down after eighteen, seven down after nineteen,

---

**Seniors: Whether you're successful in what you're doing, or fail in what you're doing, as long as you approach it with courage, you are successful. (Winston Churchill)**

five down with nine to play, all square at the thirty-sixth. I won on the thirty-seventh hole. What you don't hear so much was that the previous year in the semifinals of the same championship, Arnold Palmer beat me 8 and 6. I remember he started the afternoon round eagle, par, birdie, birdie, birdie, and I was gone! However, the sharp defeat taught me a very good lesson. It strengthened me for that match against Lema so that, even when no one would have given me a chance in a million of winning—say, after the nineteenth hole—I still kept going and played every shot as though my life depended on it. And it paid off.

## A Tough Test

THE 1969 PGA championship at Dayton, OH, is another experience I'll never forget. Before the championship, civil rights activists had placed a series of demands before the Dayton Chamber of Commerce, the tournament sponsor, threatening to "bring Dayton to its knees in embarrassment" if they weren't met. After quiet picketing through the week of the event, they evidently decided that something more drastic had to be done, and targeted me; I suppose, because of my prominence and the racial policies in South Africa, which, ironically, I oppose.

Whatever the rights and wrongs of the case, I had a tough Saturday. I started the round in second place, just a stroke behind Raymond Floyd. Then it started. They threw telephone books at my back when I reached the top of my swing. They threw ice in my face. They charged me on the greens. They threw balls between my legs when I was putting. They screamed when I was putting. I had a fourteen-inch putt on the ninth hole, and as I took the putter back, they all screamed at the same time, "Miss it!" Somehow I managed to shoot a 71, although Raymond had meanwhile played a brilliant 67, so that now I was five strokes behind. In the end, Raymond beat me by a stroke.

However, I'm telling you, *I won that PGA*. If I ever won a tournament in my life, I won that one. I can say this, I think, without boasting: No one has ever played golf so well under such circumstances, because, thankfully, no one else has had to play under such circumstances. I didn't win in the physical sense, of course, but between God and myself, I won. He had thrown me a special challenge, a heap of adversity, if you like, and I had responded as well as I knew how. *That's winning.*

That's all that God expects of us—to try to meet the challenge with courage, and do the best we can.

Now, Will Grimsley, one of the writers there at the PGA, asked me, "Gary, why don't you simply quit playing this week? You know it's not a matter of life or death." And I replied to him, "To me, Will, it's more important than life or death." I feel strongly that God puts us on earth with various talents, just as the parable in the Bible tells us. It's up to us to use our talents —whatever the circumstances. If we don't, if we bury our talents in the ground, we'll answer for it on the last day. God gave me a talent for golf. So, for me there was no other answer.

Thankfully, I could also feel that my conscience was clear. I love all people—whatever their race. I feel that we have some terrible policies in South Africa, which I'm against and which I have done my best to change. In 1971, for example, I invited Lee Elder to play in South Africa. He came, despite overwhelming pressure not to come, and helped me eradicate apartheid in sports. That took tremendous courage on Lee's part. Another man who has come to South Africa and contributed to change is Lee Trevino. Personally, I have more respect for these two gentlemen, who were not afraid to contribute, than for the many players who obviously were afraid to get involved, and have stayed safely away.

## "MAJOR" ADVERSITY

MORE recently, I faced adversity of a different sort in my pursuit of the senior majors. I won my first major in 1986, the Senior PGA, and really I'm most thankful to God for allowing me that one, because, in so many ways, the first one is the most difficult.

As always in a major, we were playing on a very difficult course—the Champions Course at the PGA National in Palm Beach Gardens, FL, the same course where they played the 1987 PGA Championship. If you watched the latter championship on TV, you'll appreciate how easy it was to lose two or even three strokes on just one hole there. Then, there was the mental pressure, like standing on the edge of a precipice for four days. You knew that if you let the opportunity slip, then you still hadn't got your first one! I was leading by seven strokes after the second round, over Lee Elder, but at the finish, I only won by two strokes. That's what pressure can do!

A lot of players will tell you, "Major championships don't mean that much to me." However, you usually find that is because they've never won one! Believe me, if you want to get endorsements out of golf, then the majors are what you have to win, those "big ones." Even if they were played on routine courses, they would be difficult enough, because you want to win them so badly. Of course, they're in fact always played on tough courses, which are then made more difficult by narrowing the fairways, letting the rough grow, and setting the pins in tough positions. They're the ultimate test of your shot-making ability.

If you doubt what I'm saying, consider all the fine players who have failed to win one out of the four majors. Sam Snead has never won the U.S. Open. Lee Trevino has never won the Masters. Arnold Palmer never won the PGA, and now Tom Watson is in the same position.

Of course, I've had my disappointments in majors just like anyone else. In the 1986 U.S. Senior, at Scioto CC in Columbus, OH, I was in very good position to win, but bogeyed two of the last four holes with 9-irons in my hand to finish second by a stroke to Dale Douglass. This defeat was a big blow to me at the time. However, ultimately it really helped me because it made me so determined to win in 1987, which thankfully, I was able to do.

Then, there was the unfortunate scheduling of the British Open the very next week, which I have already described. However, this has made me even more determined to win the British!

I could go on, but I think that's enough to show that God will *always* send us adversity. It's up to us how we respond to it. We can go into a blue funk, give up, quit, or, as Billy Graham taught me to do, we can say, "Thank you, God, for giving me this challenge. I'll show you what I'm made of," and respond with courage, enthusiasm, and even joy.

One thing I've found in my own life is that God, in his wisdom, never sends us more adversity than we are equipped to handle. That's most important. Adversity is part of God's plan for us. We must trust him in this, as in everything else.

I have always believed that God has guided me. Here I was, a small man, from a small country, and I've been able to beat some of the finest golfers in the world—the Americans—on their home turf. Most of them have had far more advantages than I had—such as the opportunity to play college golf. I have been fortunate to have felt His presence in my life, and know I couldn't have achieved any of my goals without His aid.

I would hasten to add that I never, never pray that I may win. I just ask for courage, and to be able to do my best in everything I try to do. I think it was Winston Churchill who said, "Whether you're successful in what you're doing, or fail in what you're doing, as long as you approach it with courage, you are successful." That's the type of approach that all of us seniors should take to heart. It's worth pointing out that Churchill was sixty-five years old when, in 1940, he was called to lead the British nation against the Nazi threat. I should correct myself—he wasn't sixty-five years old, he was sixty-five years *young!*

Another great saying is one by General Douglas MacArthur: "You build courage when courage seems to fail. You regain faith when there is little cause for faith, and create hope, when hope is lost. Learn to laugh, never forget to cry. Be serious, but don't take yourself seriously."

One can't put it any better than that.

## MENTAL TECHNIQUES

ONE of the most important differences between young and older people is that the young live for today and tomorrow while older folk too often live for yesterday. So, to keep yourself young in mind, you've got to use every technique available.

The techniques that follow are, for the most part, drawn from my own experience. Although I've talked to many sports psychologists over the years, and think they do fine work—indeed, my son Wayne recently worked with one of them—they're not for me. I learned these techniques from hard work, not so much from reading. In fact, I think the finest sports psychology counseling you can get is what used to be called "The school of hard knocks."

---

**Seniors: Don't get caught up in merely reading or thinking about self-improvement. As one yoga master put it, "An ounce of practice is worth several tons of theory!"**

The experience of most of the great players in history supports this thinking. Harry Vardon didn't have a sports psychologist to go to. Neither did Ben Hogan, Lee Trevino, Sam Snead, Arnold Palmer, or Jack Nicklaus. Yet, there are few people who have used their minds better, and all from hard work.

However, don't get me wrong. I'm not saying that study and reading aren't of value. I'm not an avid reader myself, but believe that reading is as important for the mind as exercise is to the body. But, believe me when I say this, you're going to get far more out of the hard work you put into these techniques than by reading or thinking about them; in the words of one of the great yoga masters, Swami Shivananda, "An ounce of practice is worth several tons of theory."

## YOUR GOALS

TO keep progressing as a golfer or as a person, to have something to live for today and tomorrow, you've got to have goals. They give you that "something to look forward to" that is so vital a part of staying young.

There are three rules for making goals that are important:

Rule Number One is: Write them down on a piece of paper. In this way, you'll find yourself forced to follow Rule Number Two: Make your goals specific; and Rule Number Three: Make your goals practical.

For example, let's say you're an experienced senior, with twenty or thirty years of golf under your belt, and your present handicap has settled around fourteen strokes. A goal of "I'm going to take ten strokes off my game by the end of this year" is maybe one of the first to come to mind. That's fine. You should always aim high. However, once you write it down, you see how impractical it is—for the immediate future. Further, it's nonspecific, in that you haven't spelled out *how* you're going to do this. Obviously, you must do some more thinking.

After a little while, you realize that this goal is the final goal —for now—that you want to reach, but to get there, you need some intermediate goals, specific steps you can take that will help you accomplish it. For example, through analyzing your game, you might figure out that you need to improve the consistency and strength of your swing as well as your short game. So, you reschedule your final goal for, say, two years down the road. Then, put in some intermediate goals such as: 1. Instituting a weekly program of work with the heavy club, and 2. Analyzing your short game, establishing standards you want to reach, taking some lessons and setting aside time for practice.

Those intermediate goals are what keep you going toward your final goals. As you achieve them, they give you a reward, a sense of self-accomplishment. For example, when I first traveled abroad in 1955 to play golf in Europe and later America, one of my final goals was to win all four majors. However, I had to put all sorts of intermediate steps in this ladder upward. For example, I had first to make the cut in tournaments, then learn how to play well on the weekends, become a top-ten finisher, then win a tournament—any tournament—before I could expect to win a major. For you, the equivalent might be to win your flight in the club championship.

Another point I've mentioned before, but it certainly bears repeating, is you must keep adjusting your final goal, especially when you're getting close to accomplishing it. As I said earlier, you want "goals on top of goals." Otherwise, reaching your goal will cause you to be rudderless, because you don't have anything further to strive for—at least until you set another goal!

We see a lot of this in professional golf, where a young man will sometimes break through and win a PGA Tour event, then "do nothing" for several months, or even the rest of the year. This usually means that he'd set his final goal at winning a PGA Tour event, but with no backup goals to sustain further advances. Don't make this mistake!

## Visualize Your Goals

EARLIER in this book, I described how you should visualize each and every shot you make. Equally well, you've got to "see" your goals happening in your mind's eye for them to become a fact.

I have always worked hard at this facet of the mental game. Perhaps, one of the most remarkable examples of this in my own career occurred before the U.S. Open of 1965 at Bellerive CC, St. Louis, MO. For years before, I had imagined myself winning this championship, having a par 4 on the last hole to win, playing the hole, holing out, making the speech at the presentation, holding up the trophy for the photographers. Then, a most peculiar thing happened just before the championship started. By the first tee, there was a big scoreboard, which listed all the names of the previous winners in gold letters. The last one said, "1964: Ken Venturi." Then, in the space below, it said "1965," followed by a blank. The first time I walked past that scoreboard, I saw the letters "1965: Gary Player," with each letter in gold exactly like the rows above. Every time I went by that scoreboard, I looked at it, and each time I saw the same thing. And I did win that championship, in a play-off over Kel Nagle, of Australia. The only way I can explain this experience is that I must have done such a good job visualizing victory that I had self-hypnotized myself into seeing what I did see.

I had a similar experience at the 1987 U.S. Senior Open. I did a lot of visualization before that championship. In practice rounds, I visualized every shot that I would have to play. That's why I stuck to my plan of hitting 1-irons off the tees where I had to have great accuracy. Also, of course, there wasn't any pressure on me to change my plan. Anyway, on the final practice day, I went out onto the eighteenth green, and nobody was there. I saw myself playing the last hole—you might need a four to win, and this is what you'll have to do, this is the shot you'll have to hit, and I ended up by seeing myself getting the trophy. For a moment there, the visualization became quite real to me: I *was* standing there receiving the trophy. Again, I guess self-hypnosis is the only explanation that makes sense.

I'm telling you these things because I think it shows the extent to which you can take this visualizing of your goals. Of course, you won't win every match just because you visualize winning. However, I'll say this: You have a far better chance of success if you do it, and do it strongly, then if you have fuzzy goals and don't work at them.

I should add one point of a practical nature. Notice that I do my visualizing of winning *before* the tournament starts. When I'm actually playing in the tournament, I leave this final goal on a "back burner," so to speak, in my mind. My immediate concentration is focused on the next shot I'm going to play.

## CONCENTRATION

I'VE just touched on perhaps the most important aspect of concentration, and that is to stay in the present. You must not look forward to the next hole, let alone the result at the end of the round. You mustn't get ahead of yourself, but equally important, don't look backward.

I find that too many seniors tend to do that in at least two ways. So watch out for them.

The first way is when you play a bad shot. If you're still thinking about that bad shot for two, even three holes after that, you're dead. This is because your mind is in the wrong place, in the past, rather than on the here and now. Instead, tell yourself that the bad shot is over and done with. It's gone, and there's nothing you can do about it. If you find yourself in trouble because of it, then concentrate all your energies on how you can recover. Accept the challenge of the poor lie, look at it carefully, feel the wind, consider the distance, figure out what you can do—these practical considerations will bring your mind back to that next shot; in other words, you're concentrating well again.

The second way of getting stuck in the past is after a good shot, or a good hole, say, where you scored a natural birdie. If you don't watch yourself, your mind can dwell on that good shot or hole and, again, your mind is not where it should be. You've got to learn to "let go" of that good shot, or hole, and get back to your immediate task: the next hole or the next shot.

Sometimes, you'll find that a good shot—or a bad shot—can make your emotions go haywire—they're going up and down like a yo-yo and there doesn't seem to be a way to stop it. Then try this: Imagine that there's a thermometer in your throat that registers joy at the high end and misery at the low end. Your task is to keep the mercury right in the middle—neither too high nor too low. It works for me.

Occasionally, you'll find that your mind wanders away from the next shot against your wishes. If this happens to you, then again do something practical. If my mind starts gathering wool after playing a tee shot on a par 4, immediately I'll start pacing off the length of my drive. I'll actually count the yards. Say, I've hit the ball 250 yards. So, then I can see I have so many yards left into the green. The wind's coming from right to left. You see what's happening? Pacing off the drive started the whole process of thinking about the next shot, and my mind became focused in the right place before I knew it. I find that's a great help.

There's no doubt in my mind that one of the worst mistakes you can make in regard to concentration is to try to work on your game while playing. A lot of seniors make that mistake. They try to "keep the head still," or "keep the left arm straight," or whatever. This is usually fatal, again because their mind is in the wrong place. They may succeed in keeping their head still, but meanwhile they often forget to look at the ball, and blow the shot! The time to work on your game, and experiment with swing keys, is on the practice ground. Out on the course, as I said earlier, you want to stay in the visual sense; in other words, visualize the shot you want to make, the swing that will make that happen, then come back to the ball and make that same swing you just saw in your mind.

Remember: Your mind can't be in two places!

Actually, I've already given you one of the best keys to staying sharp on the golf course, and that is, simply, to enjoy yourself. I remember that coming into the 1987 U.S. Senior Open, I was in a very good frame of mind. I was having a lot of fun with the game, and as a result concentrating very well.

The previous week, I was competing in the American Express Championship at the Greenbrier, White Sulphur Springs, WV. I was on the tenth hole, and Charlie Sifford was playing the eleventh, and Charlie knocked his ball right into the hole for a hole in one. So he said to me, "Laddie, let me see you top that!" So I went over to shake his hand, and asked him how many aces he'd made, and he said, "Now, I've had ten." I replied, "Well, I've had ten, too. So, the next one of us who gets a hole in one gets a cigar!" (Charlie, you should realize, always plays with a cigar in his mouth, although I can't ever remember seeing him light it.) Anyway, a little later, I knocked my ball right into the cup with an 8-iron on the seventeenth hole!

Not content with that, the next week, during my first practice round for the U.S. Senior Open, I hit a 5-iron right into the cup on the 200-yard second hole. I had had two holes in one in four holes! And you know what happened then: I played some of the best golf in my life and won.

Arnold Palmer had a similar experience not so long ago. He had two holes in one on the same hole on successive days in the 1986 Chrysler Cup. Arnold was in marvellous spirits that week and the American team, which he captained, gave the International Team, of which I was captain, quite a shellacking, I remember—they scored 68 ½ points to our 31 ½ points.

Now, I'm not saying that you're going to win every match or even get a hole in one by enjoying your golf. However, I do say happy golf is usually good golf. If you're having fun, you'll usually play up to your potential, win or lose.

One problem a lot of seniors ask me about is that sometimes they totally lose concentration over the ball. They'll hit a very bad shot—sometimes almost whiffing it. They'll say, "I don't know what happened, but I don't remember seeing the ball after I took my address." If you experience this type of "mental blackout," here's a yoga exercise that will help you extend the time you can concentrate.

The best object of concentration is a lighted candle. (However, you can substitute a naked light bulb if a candle is not available.) Before you begin, find a quiet place where you won't be disturbed. Place the candle on a table a few feet in front of you and light it. Then, just relax in a chair and look at the flame. Fix your gaze steadily on it. Don't look at anything else, not the candle itself, the wall behind it, or any other object. Don't stare, however, and don't tense up. Stay calm, relaxed, breathe naturally and look at the flame.

Let about a minute pass. Then close your eyes. In the darkness you've created, you should be able to see an image of the candle flame in your mind's eye. (If you can't, open your eyes and look at the flame again, repeating the instructions above.) The image will roughly resemble the outline of the original flame. Keep this image steady and at a point about between your eyes. The object of the exercise is to try to retain the image of the flame as long as possible. Eventually, of course, you won't be able to stop the image darkening and you'll lose it. However, with a little practice, you'll find that you can retain the image for several minutes.

When you reach that point, I don't think you'll have much difficulty keeping your eye on the ball for the duration of the swing, which is less than two seconds!

## MEDITATION

I'M a great believer in meditation. I do it anywhere, any time that I have a few minutes of privacy. I do it in planes, lying on the floor, sitting in a chair. I just relax and meditate. I thoroughly recommend it.

---

**Seniors: Never say to yourself, "I can't putt any more." All you'll do is make yourself into a bad putter! Instead, say, "I'm a great putter—look at that putt I holed on this hole, that hole." Remember: We are what we think we are.**

I think the most valuable type of meditation is one with a subject. However, the actual subject will vary, depending on my needs. For example, if I'm "down," then I meditate on all the things I have to be thankful for. If I feel a side of my character needs work, then I meditate on that. And so on.

If I'm meditating on golf, it could be one of several different things, too.

If I need to work on my putting, for example, I might imagine myself on a practice green with two balls, and I'll tell myself the feel of the stroke I want, or practice a type of putt I've been having trouble with. It might be that my swing needs work and then I'll work on swing keys. If I've just completed my round, I replay the round in my mind. I try to realize where I've made mistakes, and learn from them. Then, I'll go on to working on my game plan for the next day, and rehearse how I'm going to play each hole, each shot.

As you can see, I'm not a believer in meditating on nothing, as is sometimes recommended. To me, at least, that's idle time. One thing I can tell you for certain, from my own experience: If you put your meditation time to constructive use, you'll derive incalculable benefits from it.

## SELF-TALK

EARLIER, I mentioned how as a young man I stood in front of a mirror and repeated out loud, "I'm the greatest golfer in the world." I know the value of this "self-talk," and am quite certain it has contributed importantly to any success I've had. Here's why.

When we talk to ourselves, in fact we're talking to our subconscious. That's the part of us where our self-image is formed. The subconscious doesn't reason—it pretty much accepts what we tell it. Basically, what we tell ourselves goes straight into our subconscious, these thoughts form a self-image, and then the subconscious works very, very hard to make this self-image come true. Therefore, if you keep on telling yourself that you're a lousy driver or putter, or whatever, *that is what you'll ultimately be*. Equally well, if you tell yourself that you're a good driver or a great putter, these things ultimately will also come true. Believe me, your subconscious will find a way to do this!

I thoroughly recommend using positive self-talk to help

achieve your goals. I still work with the mirror on occasion—whenever, in fact, I think I have the need for it. You must believe in yourself. This isn't conceit. It's confidence, it's a trust in yourself, and your swing, and your game. As I've indicated, it's a technique that can literally work wonders for you.

However, there's another side to self-talk and that's what we say about ourselves to other people. You've got to learn to control this, too, and keep it positive.

When I'm asked how I'm playing, I've always tended to answer, "Better than ever in my life!" If I don't feel this way, then who is going to feel it for me? Some people haven't liked my tendency to do this, but I think it's essential to take this positive attitude. If you say, "I'm playing badly," you'll play badly. If you don't believe me, try it. You won't say it for long!

I must admit that, when I first started to control my self-talk in this way, it was done deliberately. Now, I've trained myself to where positive self-talk is automatic. I don't consciously set the process in motion. It just happens. It can work for you in the same way.

I even do it now when I'm talking to my wife, Vivienne, or so she tells me! Here's how Vivienne recently described my positive self-talk.

"You do more of that than anyone I ever met. You come off the course, and I might say to you, 'You didn't putt very well.' Immediately, you'll reply, 'What's that? Look at the great putts I holed on the second, fifth, and ninth holes!' *You never bring yourself down.* Even if you shoot 76, you'll say, "If I'd holed those putts on the fifteenth and seventeenth, and if the ball hadn't bounced into the water on the tenth, I'd have had a good round. Tomorrow, I'll shoot 66."

Guilty, as charged!

However, the most marvellous example of what can happen as the result of positive self-talk occurred a few years ago during the 1965 Australian Open at Kooyonga GC in Adelaide. Jack Nicklaus and I were rooming next door to each other. The first day, I shot 62, and Jack shot 66. Coming back to the hotel, he says to me, "How on earth can I shoot 66 and be four strokes behind! Tomorrow, I'm going to catch you, you little so-and-so!" And he did. The next day, Jack shot 63, and I shot 70. On the way back to the hotel that evening, I say to him, "How can I shoot 132 for two rounds—an average of 66—and be three strokes behind! Big guy, I'm going right past you tomorrow!" The third day, Jack sent his caddie over as I left the tenth green. I told him that I was 10 under—for the round! I shot 62, and went on to win with a 264, still a record. However, the important point is that Jack and I literally talked ourselves into playing so well.

Note also that we had a lot of fun doing it!

Trust me. Try positive self-talk and this sort of experience can happen to you, too. Maybe you don't have the skill to shoot 62s and 63s as Jack and I did, but your performance *will* improve, whatever your level of skill. That's a promise.

## CHAPTER SIXTEEN

# NOW, IT'S UP TO YOU

**I**'VE HAD ENORMOUS FUN working on this book, and I hope you, too, derive the same amount of enjoyment from reading it. I've shown you, I hope, that your game doesn't have to deteriorate as you get older. In fact, if you'll work on your exercises, both physical and mental, acquire the "Walk-Through" swing, and learn to draw the ball, you can keep up with the youngsters, and beat them when you have a good day. I've discussed the technique of just about every conceivable shot. Now, it's up to you to put it all into practice.

If there was one thought I'd like to leave you with it would be this: *Stay productive.* Time is getting shorter, so make these golden years count!

This advice comes from a man who never went to school, yet I have learned so much from him. I mean, of course, Willie Betha, the foreman on my ranch. As I've said, he's at least sixty-five, and I've known him since 1964, when I bought the ranch.

To me, Willie is like a father and a brother, all in one. I've assured him that, whenever he wants to stop working, he can. I've promised him he'll have the house I built for him free and clear, plus a pension. But he's an incredible guy. He prefers to keep on working! He makes a nice salary. However, that's not the reason he keeps going. As he says to me, "You've got to have productivity. You've got to work hard. I'm not a rich man, but I'm rich in that I have my health. Look at so many of your white friends who come and visit the ranch. Remember that young man who came the other day? He has a big stomach—he can't work with *me!*"

*Willie Betha and Gary Player.*

Willie takes great pride in his strength, and rightfully so. He's earned it through hard work. He is one of the happiest people I know, with the biggest smile you'll ever see. He's happy because he loves what he's doing, his body is in great shape, and his productivity is good.

I've taken these lessons to heart in my own life and I hope you will in yours.

However, productivity for one person is not necessarily productivity for another. It's "different strokes for different folks."

For example, I see a man like Arnold Palmer. In his own mind, he thinks he's lucky. He's a happy man, and that's the most important thing. After playing in golf tournaments or exhibitions, he goes back to his home, which is on a golf course, and every day he'll play golf with his friends. He loves to do it and that's great. It's not that Arnold doesn't have other interests. His family life is very important to him, he loves to fly and has many business interests. However, Arnold normally likes to get his business out of the way in the morning. If he can't tee it up come the afternoon, he's not too happy!

However, that is not good for me. I'm a different type of person. I need diversion. When I get home, I don't want to go out and play golf every single day. I do play golf with my friends, but by no means every day. Many days, I don't want to play golf at all. Harry Vardon, I remember, once warned against becoming "overgolfed." This is certainly true for me. I need to recharge my batteries doing many different things.

I want to work in the stables, I want to ride, I want to put up fences, and cut hay. I take a great interest in the genetic side of raising horses. I'm very interested in the hydroponic methods we use on our farm to grow food. I think this last is so important, because in the future, with world overpopulation a real threat, this technology may be essential.

I also love nature. That's another thing that Willie Betha and I have in common. In the morning sometimes, he'll say to me, "Listen to that turtle dove," or "What a beautiful rain we had last night. That ground was very thirsty. Today, the ground is not thirsty any more." We'll pass by a place where they're burning wood on the farm, clearing some land, and he'll say, "Smell that smoke!" He's so aware of his surroundings, it's amazing. One evening recently, there was the most beautiful sunset and he and I just sat down and drank it in. No words were necessary. He has a richness because of his closeness to nature that to me is so far beyond a man who has ten million dollars in the bank but lives in a big city and inhales smog and pollution every day. That man may have material things, but he doesn't have a fraction of what a person who lives in and loves the countryside enjoys.

I think one of the reasons I'm so productive and playing so well on the Senior Tour is because I've been so closely associated with nature. I draw a lot of strength from it and it gives me a peace and a philosophy that's unbeatable.

For example, I have said that facing adversity with courage and turning it into a positive force is one of the great virtues. You can see the very same thing in nature. The cactus bush grows out in the desert, with little water. It faces a harsh sun, and a cruel winter, and thrives. Out of that adversity comes some of the most beautiful flowers you'll ever see. There's God reminding you that nothing can survive without adversity. That's why I'm a such a great lover of the cactus.

Working with nature is one of the main reasons why I'm so interested in golf course architecture. I want to leave something beautiful behind me that other people can enjoy in the future.

At any rate, the point I'm making is that everyone's different. It's up to you to take what I've said, and make it your own. Work with it the way that suits you best. You've got to set your own goals, and work on them until they're fact. Then go onto your next goal, and so on.

Above all, I hope you'll make a point of enjoying your golf, while realizing that nothing will happen unless you make some sacrifices, and are prepared to put time into working on what we've discussed.

For example, I won the 1968 British Open at Carnoustie. However, I shot 74/71 the first two rounds, and obviously things weren't going too well. I kept telling myself that everyone who plays is going to have bad times. I kept my patience and went out to the practice tee at 10:30 that night (in summer, it's still light in Scotland at that time of night). Believe it or not, I found a little something that really seemed to help me, and I went on to win by two strokes over Jack Nicklaus and Bob Charles!

If you want to get the most out of what I've told you, there's no doubt that working hard, going that "extra mile," will help make your dream a reality. Always keep in mind one of my favorite sayings, which is applicable to many pursuits, but particularly to golf: "The sire of confidence is practice."

Lastly, to be as productive as possible, an essential ingredient is to get organized! I know this to be the case in my own life, and I'm sure the same applies in yours.

I'd like to repeat a thought I first mentioned in the exercise chapter, and extend it here to everything we've discussed. As I said, whether you work in a business or are a homemaker, I'm sure you make lists, plan your schedule, and so on. You need this discipline to get things done.

Apply the same thinking to all I've given you in this book. Figure out your best time to exercise, meditate, visualize, practice, and play. Make up a schedule, and stick to it as far as possible. You'll never regret it.

The rewards are there, believe me. If you keep the characteristics of youth—a forward-looking, strong mind in a supple, strong body—your chronological age won't matter. You'll be productive as long as the good Lord wills it, and no one can ask for more than that.

Remember: It's a lot more cheerful and hopeful to be seventy years young than to be forty years old!

# INDEX